From Hollywood With Love

From Hollywood With Love

BESSIE LOVE

ELM TREE BOOKS
Hamish Hamilton · London

First published in Great Britain, 1977
by Elm Tree Books Ltd
90 Great Russell Street, London WC1B 3PT
Copyright © 1977 by Bessie Love

SBN 241 89342 9

Some of the material in this book originally appeared in the
following articles which the author wrote for *The Christian
Science Monitor*: 'Embers of Soul-Fire', 'Hollywood Wildlife',
'Moonlighting for Sundown', 'Broadway Melody
Remembered', 'Hollywood Reviewed', 'Tears on Command',
'Sister of Six', 'The Well-Groomed Bride', 'Perils of
Pronounciation', 'An Aryan'.

Typeset by Filmtype Services Limited, Scarborough
Printed in Great Britain by Ebenezer Baylis & Son Ltd,
The Trinity Press, Worcester, and London

Introduction

BESSIE LOVE HAS A LOT TO answer for as far as I am concerned. Born too late for the silent era, I was nevertheless fascinated with it from an early age, thanks to the early films I cranked through my toy projector. One of these was missing its title; it was a fragment of a silent feature, and it starred Bessie Love. I knew it was Bessie Love because my parents recognized her at once. The film, in this truncated form, made little sense, but I was struck by Bessie Love as soon as I saw her. Although the film was very old, there was nothing dated or old-fashioned about its star. She was extremely beautiful, of course – but so were most Hollywood stars. Bessie Love had a quality which surprised me, a quality of immediacy and freshness which set her apart from anyone else in the picture. I wouldn't use the word as a compliment now, but then, being a schoolboy more interested in the current cinema than in forgotten silents, I thought of her as 'modern'.

The more I mentioned the name, the more reaction I got. Bessie Love had obviously made a deep impression on a great many people. I went to the local library and looked her name up in their one book on film history (Bardeche and Brasillach's *History of the Film*), but she was described simply as 'the exquisite little girl with the round head'.

A few years later, when I was sixteen, I spotted the name Bessie Love among the cast on a poster for a stage play. There could hardly be any connection – after all, what was a Hollywood star doing at the Embassy Theatre, Swiss Cottage? But I wrote a letter just in case, and asked this Bessie Love if she was that Bessie Love, and, to my unparalleled delight, received a reply:

'The film you describe must be *A Sister of Six*, which was the first starring film I made. It was directed by the Franklin Brothers – Sidney and Chester. Mr Sidney Franklin has become a very important film

5

producer as you probably know if you are that interested in films. With your very kind permission, and if it would not inconvenience the entire household, I would like to see the film.'

Kind permission! Inconvenience!! Seldom have those words been greeted with such astonishment. I was thrilled to bits – the only problem being that of anti-climax. I had neglected to explain that my film was a brutally abridged version of the original; instead of the full hour and a quarter, Bessie Love would see the whole story whip by in less than seven minutes. Never mind. This was a great opportunity. My parents were as impressed as I was at the thought of meeting one of their favourite Hollywood stars, and we were a trifle nervous on the appointed afternoon. What does one say to a star? Do they take tea, or should one produce vintage claret and caviar? Apprehension had reached the nail-biting stage by the time the doorbell rang. I scurried downstairs, and escorted Bessie Love, and her daughter Patricia, up to our flat, opening the living room door with a flourish. As Bessie Love stepped forward, a heavy curtain, designed to keep out the draught, collapsed on her, pelmet, rail and all.

I cannot think of a less promising introductory moment. It looked horribly like a planned gag from a Mack Sennett comedy. How can one begin to apologize to someone who is totally enveloped in thick golden velvet? But instead of a gasp of horror we heard a giggle of amusement as we struggled to remove the curtain. To our intense relief, we discovered that Bessie Love was equipped with an irrepressible sense of humour. After that, there could be no anti-climax, and the film was greeted with further merriment and some fascinating reminiscence. I must blame this reminiscence for fuelling my growing obsession with the silent film. My notes betray my naïve enthusiasm; I knew virtually nothing about film history, and thus the smallest memory was of the greatest significance: 'Audition in *Intolerance*! Mack Sennett began with D. W. Griffith!! J. Stuart Blackton made film in wide-screen in 1925!!!'

As I realized later, these names proved that Bessie Love had had first-hand experience with the very men who created the art of film. Whenever historians are asked to list the ten greatest films ever made, *Intolerance* (1916) invariably appears near the top. It was the peak of achievement of America's greatest director, David Wark Griffith, whose studio became a training ground for some of the most outstanding actors and directors in Hollywood. Yet Griffith was not alone; other pioneers contributed vital elements to the progress of the picture business, and J. Stuart Blackton was among the most distinguished.

Think of the silent era, and you think, perhaps, of sickly sentimentality and technical crudity. But these are myths. Bessie Love's first films coincided with the first flowering of technical excellence in American films, the winning of a vast new audience and the establishment of movie-going as a world-favourite entertainment. Bessie Love played most frequently the role one might expect – that of the innocent young girl – but she invested her parts with a delicacy, honesty and intelligence that came naturally to her. She failed to overact, unlike some of the specially-imported stage stars, trained to project their performances across the footlights. She failed to overact because, she says, she didn't know how to. Nor did Mary Pickford, Lillian Gish, Blanche Sweet or Mae Marsh – all actresses who came to prominence through the films of D. W. Griffith. They shared a fragile beauty with a powerful screen presence, the impact of which was at odds with their physical presence – they were all around five feet tall. Once Griffith had caused his audience to fall in love with these girls – a few lustrous close-ups was enough to achieve that – all he had to do was to place them in dangerous situations to create enormous suspense. But as soon as one method had been tried, the next had to be more complicated. Griffith had to push forward the boundaries of cinematography to keep his audience alert and excited.

In 1912, it was enough to lock Lillian and Dorothy Gish in a room and show burglars shooting at them through a hole in the wall. But by 1915, and Bessie Love's first contact with the moving picture, Griffith considered it necessary to isolate his players in a massive reconstruction of the City of Babylon, and show them being besieged by the entire Persian army. In *Intolerance*, his camera rampaged outrageously across the centuries to encompass not only the Fall of Babylon, but the Massacre of the Huguenots, the Crucifixion and the viciousness of so-called Reform in contemporary America. The presentation of past and present on one plane was too much for the audiences of the time – who complained of Belshazzar being run down by an automobile – and before you dismiss the naïvete of the audiences of 1916, I should add that it is still too much for many audiences of today. *Intolerance* was a magnificent gesture by a great artist, and it is hardly surprising that Bessie Love retains such a profound admiration for D. W. Griffith.

Oddly enough, Bessie Love's own approach to life has a certain Griffith touch. Past and present exist for her, too, on the same plane of thought, and thus she is afflicted with neither nostalgia nor regret. As a person, she has many of the qualities Griffith most admired. He hailed her in 1915 as the most promising actress he had ever directed. Sadly, he did not direct her again, but merely supervised the films she appeared in at his studio.

Her approach to life ruled out some of the methods by which careers have been hacked out in Hollywood. After the First World War, when Hollywood had captured world markets, and virtually anything that moved made money, the top stars – Mary Pickford, Douglas Fairbanks and Charlie Chaplin – joined D. W. Griffith in forming United Artists and proclaiming their independence. Bessie Love also formed her own company. But whereas Fairbanks, Pickford and Chaplin had the most acute business brains in the industry, Bessie Love shared with Griffith a distaste for business manoeuvring, and an unqualified trust in business advisers. Although she is still loyal to her managers, and won't have a word said against them, I think they did her no good at all. Her career took a battering. As she says today, 'I started at the top and worked my way down'. The fact that she was able to return to the front rank in the face of desperate competition, is a tribute to her enormous ability.

Sadly, of all the films she made in the silent days, only a handful survive, and in that handful are few of her outstanding roles. *The Lost World* (1925) was notable more for its dinosaurs than for its thespians; Bessie Love gets a few statutory close-ups before the camera turns to the death struggle of prehistoric monsters. In *Young April* (1926) she plays a schoolgirl who suddenly discovers she's a duchess, and is courted by a Prince (Joseph Schildkraut). Bessie Love plays the role with immense charm, and it is one of the more representative of the surviving films. In *The King On Main Street* (1925) she introduced the Charleston to the screen. In *Rubber Tires* (1927) she plays the only capable member of a family struggling to cross the continent in an ancient automobile, and the picture gives her an opportunity for comedy which she uses to great effect. Apart from *The Lost World*, these were programme pictures, made quickly to fulfil a company's quota to the exhibitor. Much more demanding in terms of acting was *Human Wreckage* (1923), a picture about drug addiction, in which Bessie played a young mother, passing on her addiction to her child. The film was produced by Mrs Wallace Reid, whose husband, a very popular and talented star, had just died of drugs. 'Bessie Love's death scene,' wrote critic Harry Carr, 'devoid of theatric agony, was like a foretaste of eternal beauty, a passing into the ultimate dream.' Sadly, the picture has been lost. Lost, too, is *Sundown* (1924), a realistic western in documentary style about the passing of the great Texas cattle ranches – an appropriate role since Bessie Love was born in Texas, the daughter of a cowboy. In *Soul-Fire* (1925) (which only just survives, in a print copied so badly that the original image has all but vanished) one can see in her peformance of the native girl the qualities which caused Maurice Maeterlinck, the author of *The Blue Bird*, to declare: 'Of all who play, I like Bessie Love. She has the purest art.'

After her period of bad management, Bessie Love began to climb back. Her indelibly youthful beauty proved an obstacle, for she persisted in looking sixteen well into adulthood. Public taste, reflected at the box office, tended to favour more sophisticated and suggestive stars – such as Pola Negri. Yet audiences responded very positively to her performances. As one columnist noted in *Photoplay* in 1925: 'Though often her role was not a featured one in big productions, Hollywood has a tradition that Bessie Love will steal any picture that she is in; that she has, in fact, stolen more pictures from the people supposed to be starring in them than anyone else on the screen. It isn't quite fair to enumerate them, but if you will stop and think I'm sure you will remember half a dozen pictures from which you took away most poignantly the memory of something Bessie Love did.'

And it is not hard to think of a more recent example – the most moving scene in *Isadora* was due to Bessie Love's brilliant performance as Isadora Duncan's mother.

What about the offscreen Bessie Love? I can attest to her popularity from my experience of interviewing silent film veterans in America. Whenever I found it hard to gain the interest of these veterans, the shameless dropping of the name Bessie Love softened the heart of the most confirmed hater of interviewers. And mentioning it during an interview inevitably brought a warm glow in response. A clue to this popularity was provided by a *Photoplay* reporter who visited the windswept Texas location for *Sundown*, and found himself marooned in the crew's tent, frozen to death on a pitiless winter night. 'We were none of us very happy. We were used to our comforts. It was very cold and dismal and the uninhabited prairie outside depressed us. And then the girl, sort of casually, picked up her ukelele – dread instrument of torture as a rule – and holding it cockily under her left arm began to sing. I am not very poetic as a rule, but the thought that still comes to my memory of that evening is "a brown wren turned into a nightingale". And so she did. Bessie Love sang for us – all sorts of songs, funny little character songs that she had picked up, heaven alone knows where! – jazzy, daring, tantalizing little songs; tender, crooning things that have outlived the centuries – and we forgot the snow outside, and the penetrating cold, and the tent became a happy, congenial, friendly place where a man would rather be than almost any place he could think of.

'It takes personality to "put over" a song across the footlights. But it takes personality plus to put over a song in a tent surrounded by snow and wind and filled with hungry, cold and slightly disgruntled men.'

Popularity can survive without talent. An acting career cannot. In 1925, another columnist paid tribute to Bessie Love's talent with this remarkable statement: ' "Who is the most useful actress in the world?" I asked a casting director. "If you had to send a company away on a long trip, and they were going to make a lot of pictures, and you could only send one actress, whom would you choose?" I knew what his answer would be before I asked him – Bessie Love! Any casting director in Hollywood would give the same answer. For versatility, little Miss Love is without rivals. She can be fifteen – or fifty. She is convincing and winsome as a screen sweetheart, yet she can be almost sexless. She is one of the few women of the screen who can make you believe in pure virginal innocence and unsophistication; yet one of her best parts was that of the ruined girl in Marshall Neilan's *The Eternal Three*. In Charlie Ray's *Dynamite Smith* she also gave an astonishingly vivid and accurate picture of a prostitute in a tough dive on the Barbary Coast (actually the Yukon).'

Sound, the revolution which killed the careers of so many of the biggest stars – John Gilbert, Vilma Banky, Pola Negri, Charles Farrell – brought Bessie Love back from the obscurity of a vaudeville career to the pinnacle of success as Hank in *The Broadway Melody* (1929). And this is the part for which she is best remembered.

Wrote Harry Carr in *Photoplay*, reporting on the première: 'All the stars of the local firmament arrived at Grauman's Chinese in diamonds that dimmed the searchlights and ermine that queens could once afford. They were filmed and radioed throughout the world. Carmel Myers, school chum of Bessie, stepped up to the microphone and said: "I'm grateful for this night because Bessie Love is triumphing and if ever anyone deserved success, Bessie Love does."

'Carmel said what all Hollywood felt. And every night since there has been a hush – then a storm of applause for that great scene in which Hank sobs alone in her dressing room. I repeat what I wrote two years ago in *Photoplay*:

' "There is no finer or sweeter character on the screen than Bessie Love." '

And now, as they used to say in the movie magazine serials, please read on . . .

Kevin Brownlow

Author's Note

THE FLASH-BACK IN FILM
treatment is now passé. The new technique is cutting past, present and
future all into one continuous train of thought, one present consciousness,
making unimportant the sequence of events in the passage of time.

Though I certainly didn't do this consciously it is the way I've written
what is offered here. It may appear that I skip about in time. This is not
true. It is all of a pattern – a present pattern. There is no definite finished
past to anything for me. It flows. One thing leads to another and back
again. The golden threads and the bright red ones scamper about through
the grey, even the knots and broken ends are there – well, maybe not all of
them, but enough. And it's all one present piece. I'm still adding to it, too,
living, working, weaving away like anything!

Originally I wanted to write this book from memory only, without
correction or reference to any source outside myself, and purposely kept
away from other books of the kind for fear of not telling it as I remembered
it. I now thank those people and organisations who came to my rescue:
DeWitt Bodeen; members of my family and friends old and new scattered
over the States and abroad; George Geltzer, Anthony Slide for their help
with the filmography and Harold Dunham who compiled it; the British
Theatre Museum; Francis Day & Hunter Ltd; the Victoria and Albert
Museum; the Enthoven Collection; Mander and Mitchenson Theatre
Collection; Heather Jimenez's penetrating prods and crits ('Your father
was a cowboy? Tell it!'); Archives of the British Film Institute who kindly
allowed me to tent out for some time on their Soho premises; Performing
Rights Society; *Silent Screen* by Daniel Blum; Dennis Woodford who
bullied me into writing the thing at all; Anne Boston who made it flow,
instead of stutter; and, of course, Kevin Brownlow. For his encourage-
ment and generosity in helping to compile what material there was into a
book, I am most, most grateful. So into the deep end – here goes!

Chapter One

JUST THE OTHER DAY, WHILE looking for something else I ran across an envelope from the Fine Arts Studio, 4500 Sunset Boulevard, Los Angeles, California. A little surprised, I looked closer and read, scrawled across in pencil in my own unmistakable scratching, 'My First Day in Pictures'. In the envelope was a typesheet containing my first impressions. It was dated 4 October, 1916.

So often I'm asked what it was like 'in early films'. Well, I consider *The Great Train Robbery* to be an early film – I'm told it was made in 1903, and that's probably when, as a child, I saw it. I get pretty shirty with my inquisitors, I can tell you, until D. W. Griffith's name comes up. Then my ruffled feathers are smoothed down, we gab for a bit, I tell them 'how it was' with that wonderful man, and before I know it I'm launched into my life story.

I was born Juanita Horton, in Midland, Texas. In Britain my name is pronounced Jew-an-eeta instead of the Texan Huahn-eeta. When I learned to talk I had a Mexican nurse and could soon jabber bilingually, telling my mother, 'You wouldn't understand. That's Mexican.' Midland was a barren cow-town then. As soon as we left they struck oil and now you can't get a decent cup of water in the place. From Midland, we shuttled back and forth between ruler-flat deserts and the rockies of Arizona and New Mexico and the overpowering gardens of California, goodness knows how many times before I finished first grade at school.

My father, John Cross Horton, was born in Hot Springs, Arkansas. After an appallingly unhappy childhood, he ran away from home when his mother died. He didn't talk about it much, so I know precious little about his early life. He had no schooling – none that showed. He was always excruciatingly sensitive about this lack of education and background. His tongue tied up in knots, his brain congealed at the thought of meeting and mixing with 'ladies and gentlemen' whom he longed to 'equal'. When he walked up the aisle in rented white tie and tails to give me away at St James's Episcopal Church in Los Angeles at the end of the twinkling Twenties, I thought there was something wrong with him – he walked with measured tread as one in a trance. His complex was such a pity, because he was good fun and so relaxed with people he knew.

Many men of the wide open spaces at the beginning of the century could neither read nor write. But they could cope. They were ambitious, astute, shrewd. They learned. I've known more than one in the film industry. My father would work his feet off for anyone else – long hours meant nothing to him and he had a fantastic sense of loyalty – but for himself he could do nothing. Every penny was spent as soon as he got it. He had no judgement, he never saved or planned for the future. He was a terrible show-off with money. I'm sure it was due to his feverish sense of insecurity. We often see it around us: people doing the most outrageous things – anything – to keep from being forgotten, to prove to the world and themselves that they do exist.

Dad learned to take care of himself early and it made him pretty tough. He punched cattle in Texas, tended bar in Arizona, New Mexico and Los Angeles. But no matter where he went his feet were still in stirrups in Texas, and like a true son of that state he pronounced it, 'Texiss'.

Few of us imagine our parents as ever having been romantic. When I was about eleven or twelve I discovered in an old yellow trunk a bundle of love letters tied up in red ribbon, written by my father to my mother when they were courting. It is one of the things which endeared him to me for the rest of his life in spite of anything he did wrong. The devotion, simplicity, bad spelling and squiggly writing must have made those epistles all the more priceless to my schoolteacher mother.

Can't you picture the two of them as they drove up in a hired hack to the small-town Texan church, to get married? Demure, pretty Mother, with her deep-set eyes and quiet smile – she said it froze at the sight of a camera – her straight black hair swept up in a pompadour, leg-o'-mutton sleeves and swirling skirts of the day, carrying those precious letters in her telescope-valise. And my dashing father with his diamond stud, his six-shooter out of sight (I expect every man in the congregation was heeled), his silk handkerchieves, and his Stetson cocked on one side.

It was Thanksgiving Day and there was a service going on in the church. Still sitting in the hack, the happy couple sent in for the preacher, who told the congregation to hold on for the ceremony. But my impetuous father saw no reason to move. All they needed for a wedding was themselves and a minister, which they had. Why not perform the ceremony in the hack? Apparently nobody saw any reason why they shouldn't, so the Holy Words and promises were said then and there, Mr and (now) Mrs drove off, and the congregation was sent home. When Mother asked Dad if he'd brought his trunk, he said, 'Trunk? Hell, no! I've got a flour-sack.'

Dad's bachelor escapades continued after marriage and he made the most extraordinary practice, whatever he did, of coming home and telling

14

Mother. So next day whenever a neighbour left a trail of smoke in her haste to repeat all the details, Mother would smile and say, 'Yes, I know. Johnnie told me.'

In Arizona, when I was tiny, Dad used to take me on visits to his girlfriends. Naturally the girls made a fuss over me, for Dad was a good spender – except at home. Each girl rolled her own 'cigareets' like a man. (My father told me that he used to roll a cigarette in one hand while holding the reins of a galloping horse in the other.) The girls dabbed their faces with chamois skin, sometimes lace-edged, either to apply face powder or just to take off the shine – powder puffs came in many years later.

When I was much older, perhaps twelve, in Los Angeles, I was listening to Dad talking one day to Mrs Griffith (nothing to do with films), a pleasant stout lady who ran a beauty parlour. He used to take me there sometimes to have my hair dressed. Dad said he had taken me to places of questionable reputation when I was small, and I wondered when that could have happened – and where, and why – because by now I knew what he was talking about. Mrs Griffith was horrified and asked why he had done such a thing. He said he had wanted me to see the other side of life. But I think he'd wanted to show me off, bless his heart. He had few possessions and not many friends – other than the girls.

Dad was a bartender. He so wanted to become a 'gentleman'; he was afraid he wasn't 'going to amount to a damn!' After we'd settled in the working-class suburbs of Los Angeles and I was going to McKinley Grammar School, he used to take the streetcar at five in the morning to go to work at the Oak Bar across from the old County Court House down town, and attend night school after he finished in order to become a chiropractor (bone and muscle setter) and be called – 'Doc'!

Mother was born in Sweetwater (she always liked the film star Louise Brooks because she too came from Kansas). Mama came from an enormous family, clannish and loyal to each other. They were pioneers, coming West in waggons as far as Kansas. Those people, like all hill people, have a quality difficult to describe. An innate dignity? What they have to be dignified about is hard to imagine; but I think that's it. They are beholden to nothing on earth. They are not ill-mannered, but they would never make courtiers.

In spite of her happy farm-family youth, the soul-destroying rural poverty and body-breaking farm labour made Mother look on a cottage in the country as just this side of a strait-jacket. The crude, backwoods way of doing things gave her an aversion to anything not store-bought. She thought anything made by hand was done that way because you couldn't afford it in the shops.

Mother was slender, in delicate health – my birth nearly killed her, though in that day I don't suppose they even thought there was anything wrong with her. The mess I made of her insides put paid to any more children. We were always very close, she and I. Crossing the street once in

some city we were nearly run over. I didn't help much: the more Mother tried to push me to safety, the more I clung to her many full skirts. When we were safely up on the sidewalk she asked why I hadn't run when she told me to. I'd thought she was going to be killed and I didn't want to be left behind.

She was gentle and always turned to the Bible for help. It became worn and weather-beaten in our house. Mother could almost tell what to have for supper by opening the Good Book and reading what it said.

Since we moved around a great deal – Mexican beans never jumped faster – I was always beginning at the beginning again at school. I had barely warmed the tip-up seat of my desk in one place before I was on the Santa Fé again, heading for Williams, Albuquerque or back to Los Angeles. Finally we came to roost in Los Angeles, where Mother worked in (and managed) a succession of restaurants.

There used to be parades in town and I, for one small girl, nearly burst with excitement every time I saw one. Beautiful! With flowers, colours, lovely girls in pretty costumes and floats mounted on flat-cars, long and with no sides, which ran on the street-car lines with overhead trolleys. There were many brass bands and horses, horses, horses, with silver-mounted bridles and saddles and long western silver-mounted stirrups. In the evening of the same day, there would be an electric parade, with the floats illuminated – strung with lights from one end to the other.

In the following years, the processions became more sophisticated. While I was at Los Angeles High School I appeared on the school float one year – I was a lady-in-waiting at Queen Elizabeth's court, wearing a great brocaded costume. We'd had a popularity contest to vote for the Queen, and the runners-up – Carmel Myers was another – were ladies-in-waiting.

By the Twenties Hollywood's processions were fantastically beautiful affairs organized by wealthy firms and major studios, with all the cowboy stars riding in them. Then there was always the famous Pasadena Rose Parade on New Year's Day, which had whole tableaux sculpted in flowers and pretty girls. Traditionally the Pasadena schoolchildren used to help take care of the flowers, sprinkling them all the night before to keep them fresh. But we'd never heard of elegant Pasadena when I was a little squirt. Our flashy, brassy Main Street parades were the realization of every dream.

Los Angeles has always been a great show town. The local Burbank Theatre had a stock company (repertory), and so did the Belasco. And there was the Mason Opera House, a great barn of a place which showed all the touring companies, including very good New York ones. In one café which Mother managed, we used to place show bills on the low display areas behind the lace curtains in the windows, each side of the front door. In exchange we received complimentary tickets for seats in the galleries. (Cinemas were not yet elevated to the aristocratic class of advertisers.) With our 'comps' we went to all the shows in town – and 'we' always included me.

Except once. It was at another café one night when I considered suicide – I was perhaps eight – because they'd gone off to a theatre without me. I was chagrined at the idea of having to stay home like a child, with the waitress and her whole family to keep me company. I'd seen too many blood-curdling plays already, there's no doubt about that. I had it all figured out: I don't think I'd have accomplished much but I sure would have made a mess to be remembered.

Most of the leading actors from the Burbank Theatre went into films. Forrest Stanley and Harlan Tucker were tremendous heart-throbs. William Desmond went to Ince's studio and eventually became a cowboy pin-up. Lewis Stone and his wife Florence played *The Prisoner of Zenda* type in swashbuckling stories; Hobart Bosworth and his wife Adele Farrington appeared together. I once saw tiny Blanche Hall in *Peter Pan*; inspired, I came home and jumped off the café ice-box. I was sure I could fly – it looked so easy the way she did it. I landed in a heap on the floor with the ice drippings, and yelled. (Years later, in 1924, I was tested, like every other actress in Hollywood, for the film *Peter Pan*. It's the only test I've ever made that I was satisfied with. Unfortunately I was apparently the *only* one satisfied. All the tests were sent to Sir James Barrie in England, who had the final say. A pilgrimage was made by one or two of the aspirants, to press their claim to be the ideal elf. I don't blame them – had I thought of it, I'd have joined them. Betty Bronson finally made it.)

While we were going to the Burbank, Mother and I lived in a room above the café. I amused myself when alone there by writing with chalk on the smooth, undecorated plaster walls. I was never allowed to play with children in the street; whenever I was sent to the store I was expected to come straight back. Once I stopped with the young ones – they were *so* interesting – just outside the front door. My girlish laughter drifted aloft to our room like the smell of frying onions. Mother, in true fishwife fashion, stuck her head out, said her piece, and I was soon inside looking out.

On another occasion I was playing alone on the lawn of the old Court House, which was slightly elevated on the corner of the next block down the hill from us. On the ground floor, with long open windows with heavy black bars reaching to the outside walks, was a gaol or room where young prisoners awaited trial. I was playing outside these windows near the big date-palm which spread over the lawn in front of the building. (This tree, which I thought magnificent, was removed while we were living in the neighbourhood and a statue of Stephen M. White erected instead. I'm sure now it was better to commemorate such a fearless citizen, but I wasn't at all sure at the time.) From my play place a young prisoner called

19

With Father and Mother in 1926 in front of the Ambassador Hotel, Los Angeles, where we then lived

me over to the iron bars. He asked me to get some Fig Newtons – a kind of pastry bar filled with figs. He gave me the money through the iron bars and I ran down the lawn, over to Temple Street, bought the cookies, brought them back and passed them through the bars to him.

Hollywood was a small town when I was buying Fig Newtons on Temple Street. It's not even mentioned in my old school geography book; nor the film industry in the economic section, which is all dairies and orange groves. Most of the hills above Hollywood were not yet opened for building development, and had no roads or lighting, gas or water for homes and estates.

There were lots of parks. Sycamore Grove was a favourite, a natural park north of Los Angeles where we used to take picnics with friends. We children were allowed to wade in the clear, fresh, cold creek running through the grove and gather loads of watercress.

With the move to our last restaurant in L.A. I started growing up. I had a couple of restless nights. Once, when I was a little faint, Mother discovered I'd gone to bed wearing my newly-permitted waspie. Another night the headache was found to be caused by my hair, which I had dressed high, and heavy, with pins: I had gone to bed without removing a single one.

My first 'heels' were purchased when Mother and I went to town for high button shoes which all the girls were wearing. The shoe salesman explained that my father had already been in and picked out some footwear for me. Then he showed them to us: Mary Janes – flat, baby-doll, one-strap. I brushed aside these little-girl offerings and went out shod like my contemporaries, swinging my hips to prove I could although not permitted to do so.

I had begun attending McKinley Grammar School, and once started, in the Sixth Grade, I stayed right up to my Freshman year before leaving to join L.A. High, way down town. (Now McKinley is called Carver Junior High; all the neighbourhood is black and the entire school district in which we were all scattered is included in Watts. When we were children Watts was a tiny suburb some distance out of town.)

The hours of Los Angeles High School were the usual nine to three. I went from eight to four – one hour extra in the morning, another after school, and no free study periods which everyone else had. I nearly made the four-year course in two. Why the rush? Why the breakneck speed to get through school, which I loved (later, I used to cry when I passed it on my way to the studio), and hurtle through college? Because I planned to be a teacher. My mother had been; the pattern was already set. Although my father felt for some reason it was below my station to work for wages, 'Being a teacher's different,' he said. 'Everyone respects a teacher.' I knew one would be addressed as 'Miss' instead of 'Hey, you!', and though one would probably starve, one would do so with dignity. I didn't become a teacher. An odd chain of events brought me to films instead.

Chapter Two

IT SEEMS THAT ACTING WAS ONE thing I did *not* want to do as a child, yet several times I came near enough the burning flame of Fortune to get singed. Once I was alone for a minute in the waiting-room of a station. A lady came up and asked if I would like to go on the stage. I said, 'No', and she left. When Mother came back, I told her about the stranger's question. Mother asked why on earth I didn't want to go on the stage? I said, well, maybe I did after all. And she took the station apart trying in vain to find the lady. It was typical that Mother should accept such an offer as perfectly natural – no training, no preparation, not even an inquiry on our part. All that was needed for a stage career was my permission, which I had not deemed it fit to grant.

In those days the five-and-ten-cent stores and all the big department stores had a Sheet Music Department, with a ragtime pianist to bang out any number you wished to hear. Everyone now has a television set; everyone then had a piano. Even we did. While I was going to McKinley, we bought a brand-new upright and I took lessons. I played 'Clover Blossoms' and 'Traumerei' day and night with the windows wide open.

My friend Marguerite Lander was learning the saxophone with a Mr Parmagianni, and I accompanied her. We were given a chance to play in a musty little cinema in the middle of town. I wore my best dress which someone had given us – white net and lace, with a long waistline somewhere below the hips, and a sash. My hair was in long curls. (Everyone wore Mary Pickford curls then; they were made by curling your hair around long rags, then criss-crossing the divided ends back up, tying them firmly at the top and sleeping on them. We thought curly hair was prettier – not that it made us into film stars, or even look like them. But, although I really hadn't given it much thought, maybe we were all – including me – beginning to copy our screen favourites. I cut out all their magazine pictures, I know, and ruined my bedroom wall pinning them up.)

With silent films there was always a live musical accompaniment matching the action on the screen: chase music for Jack Pickford on horseback; romantic music for Maurice Costello; sad music for Blanche Sweet; mysterious music for Pearl White, etc, etc. Marguerite and I didn't do it that way. Mr Parmagianni had been teaching us 'Star of the East' from *Tannhäuser*. That's what we played, no matter what was happening on the screen. We didn't *know* what was happening on the screen! We were far too busy reading our music and coming out even. And when we did finish, we stopped for a breath or two, as you would if you were giving a concert, genteelly mopping hands and brow.

The manager of the small theatre came chasing up our shaky stairway, which was more like a ladder and handrail, to our thrown-together balcony overlooking the audience. He frantically motioned us to resume: 'Get moving!' he hissed. 'Begin! Play! Play!' We'd been playing without a break for hours. He said we must never stop as long as the films were running. They were non-stop. We were not asked to perform again.

For years we had been exhaustingly, drably poor. Never starving, no physical cruelty: nothing so colourful. At last my patient, saintly mother lost her temper – I can count on two fingers and a thumb the times that had happened. This time she was combing her long fine black hair, which tangled easily, and the comb got caught. 'Drat the thing!' said Mother. 'Oh, I'm so sick of us never having any money, always being in debt, living in a land of plenty and not even affording a telephone.' She pulled the comb out, hair and all, and threw it across the room, where it broke. I, slightly hysterical, laughed; I could hardly wait to tell Dad when he came in. To my surprise it made him furious. 'Why did she lose her temper?' he stormed, losing his – a blazing one. Though Mother was not in the room, he raged, threw things and slammed drawers and doors. Then I, little, insignificant, obedient, mousy *me*, lost mine, gaining strength as I went along. It was splendid! I told my delinquent father a few home truths – quite a few – which were probably none of my business, but nonetheless put to him with a clarity unmatched, I should think, in his entire experience. After which, with head high, I marched off to school and didn't notice that I had no dicky in the front of my blouse until I reached the streetcar stop and had to pin in my handkerchief.

For how many days the state of siege continued, I cannot remember, but it mattered a great deal. Mother hid Dad's gun, for one thing. Then one night, she gently suggested, 'Go in and kiss him goodnight.' I did. That's all: we never mentioned the incident again, ever.

But there was still rebellion in the air. Ma had made a decision: if we couldn't experience some of the advantages of civilization, we would go and live among the Indians. Poncie, a niece, taught them in Oklahoma and Ed, one of Ma's many brothers, taught on the reservation in Idaho. She would teach again and so would I, as soon as they'd have me.

I was preparing myself for this abrupt departure from our former way of life and about to look up the languages of the Paiutes and Shoshones, when Mother read about Mary Pickford spending the winter in Palm Beach. That did it! Only my mother could switch her sights from Paiutes to pictures. She didn't stop to inquire about Miss Pickford's qualifications for being called 'America's Sweetheart'. People were always saying that I looked like the little film actress: I, too, would enter films!

We knew my father would never consent to my hanging around a studio gate hoping to be picked up as an 'extra'. He knew quite a few extra girls. My resourceful mother said, on the Saturday before school finished for the summer, that there was no reason why I shouldn't get a job first then tell him about it afterwards. No job which took you to Palm Beach in winter could be immoral. We took it for granted that I would get it. It was just a matter of settling the trifles – which studio it would be and that sort of thing. 'Gee! Better go before school finishes. Otherwise the best jobs will be gone!' Such was my reasoning.

Mother, then working in Jantzen's Bathing Suit factory, and up for promotion to forelady, could not get away herself. So Mrs Delano, the wife of the couple renting a room from us, would accompany me to the studio where Tom Mix, cowboy star and director, made his pictures. It was in Edendale, a suburb the other side of Los Angeles. I'd been there once on a Sunday visit with my father and as Tom Mix had said I should go to see him if ever I wanted 'to get into pictures', it seemed the natural place to apply.

I had much trouble reaching Mr Mix by phone, but when I did, he told me to come out on Monday 14 June 1915, and he would see what he could do for me. Sunday night I was ill, so, without an appointment, Mrs Delano and I went to the studio on the following Saturday. But on this day Tom Mix was away, or so we were told. We were sent next door to see the Wardrobe Lady, Mrs Christian. She said, 'If you want to go into pictures you don't want to begin here. It's very rough, making cowboy pictures. Go see D. W. Griffith. He's made all the big stars.'

For the uninitiated, D. W. Griffith was the most brilliant and one of the most important film directors, producers and showmen of the film industry. This was the first time I had heard mention of him as a person, although I must have already known that he had made *The Clansman* (later called *The Birth Of A Nation*) because I had seen that with Bud Haeberle, also from L.A. High, at Clune's Auditorium and received my first compliment about looking pretty when I cried.

We felt Mrs Christian's advice made sense, so that's what Mrs Delano and I did. We took a streetcar to the studio on Sunset Boulevard in Hollywood and I asked to see Mr Griffith.

Frank Woods, head of the Scenario Department, answered my knock. I asked if I could see Mr Griffith and he asked if I had an appointment. 'Oh, yes.' (I'd been told to say that.) Meanwhile Mr Griffith, on his way to his office, overheard me and, having watched us through a slit in the door, nodded to Mr Woods for us to come in.

The great man asked all kinds of questions. My family: were they rich? My background: had I any stage experience? Studied drama? Singing? Dancing? Stage training of any kind? The answer to each question being, 'No, Sir,' he asked: Then why did I want to come into Pictures? That answer was easy: I wanted a job for the summer. Such frankness must have delighted him. Even my classmates seeking jobs as nursemaids vowed to their employers that they were taking the jobs permanently. But why did I choose acting? he asked. I think my answer to that is what got me in: 'Mama said I wasn't trained to do anything, so there was nothing left for me but acting.'

Difficult as it must have been for him to keep from guffawing, Mr Griffith didn't laugh. He never ever laughed at me, and he put other people in their place when they did. He said he would try me out and see if I *could* act and take direction. In other words, he would give me an audition – something which was rarely done in those days. He told me to go to lunch and then come back. Mrs Delano and I left his office. She was a sensible woman and concluded that our luck had been too good to risk leaving the place even for a sausage. We'd never get in again. So we'd skip lunch and wait until they got back.

The Majestic-Reliance studio in 1913 before being changed to Triangle-Fine Arts

D. W. Griffith directing Miriam Cooper in an interior shot from Intolerance. *Dorothy Gish in background, Karl Brown right*

When everybody else had eaten we went on to the open stage where they were rehearsing the Babylonian period of *Intolerance*. Henry Walthall, star of *The Clansman*, was there; Carl Stockdale was the King-Archaeologist; Tully Marshall was the High Priest of Baal who betrayed the city; George Siegmann, Cyrus; Al Paget, Belshazzar; and Signe Auen (later spelt Seena Owen), his Princess, called Beloved.

In the midst of rehearsal and before all those talented actors, I had my audition. I was supposed to be a slave girl playing with a beetle at the feet of Belshazzar. 'Watch it run away,' Mr Griffith directed, 'Go get it and bring it back . . . it's a pet. Play with it. Now put it back into the cage.' (There was no cage, of course, any more than there was a beetle. I mimed it.) 'Look up at the Prince . . . you adore him . . . he's like a god.'

Terrified of an audition? Such an attitude wouldn't have made sense to me. Shyness or self-consciousness had no part in it. If you wanted a job you went for it and either you got it or you didn't. I thought everyone had done the same thing to get their jobs. I didn't know of any difference between the standing of one actor and another in the whole theatrical business. (Once my mother asked Douglas Fairbanks if he'd been cast yet for another picture, and poor Douglas Fairbanks almost had a stroke.)

27

When rehearsal was over, Mr Griffith said to come back on Monday and they would make a screen test. I said I couldn't – I'd be at school. Patiently he asked when it would be convenient . . . We must have made some kind of deal, because the following Monday I worked as an extra, and got into terrible trouble next day at school for having been absent. I was paid $2 by the studio, which I gave to my mother, returned to school until term ended at the end of the week, had my test on Saturday as planned, got the job, and, except for some periods of unemployment, I'm *still* working in films.

A back-spot was used on my first screen test. My hair was down, which I suppose caught the light. Frank B. Good continued to be one of the best cameramen in the business long after he photographed that test. As to wardrobe, I wore my special treasure: a formal black beautifully tailored loose-weave gymnasium garment someone had given us. It had full elbow-length sleeves and wide bloomers to the knees. Perhaps this was a recent acquisition because I don't remember having worn it much for gym – but it was my pride and joy, giving me that comfortable feeling of knowing I was well dressed.

Wilfred Lucas directed the test. He was one of the older, romantic leading men for the Gishes and Mae Marsh, and was an actor of great stage and film experience. Mr Lucas gave me one piece of advice while showing me what he wanted me to do. As he stepped down into the set through the French windows at the back, he entered the spot backlight and stopped. 'You'll get so you feel when that hits you,' he said. 'Stay in it and play your scene.' He was right: you can, and do.

In the barn-like indoor stage we had Cooper-Hewitts – blue strip-lighting which cast no shadows and made everyone look like pieces of liver. There were spotlights above and standard Klieg lights on the floor – which were open! The day after working beside them, everyone wore black glasses or stayed in bed. Though we didn't know it, we were suffering from the effects of ultra-violet rays. It was years before any protection was given. The carbons, two sets to a lamp, had to be 'trimmed' every so often to make them touch after they had burned away – otherwise they would burn out in the middle of a take and squeal.

Soon all the big studios were using lights on indoor sets – but not before Ince built his new studio in Culver City in 1916, the big stage made entirely of clear glass. I don't know who designed it but can you imagine not thinking of ventilation in a place where the sun shines bright when it shines?

Open outdoor stages were just that – no walls, long and narrow, running lengthways across the front of the prop rooms and indoor stage. Sets were built across them like a grid-iron. Overlapping strips of white muslin, three to six feet wide, could be drawn on wires, like so many clothes lines, from the building out over the sets like awnings, thus diffusing the light in each without disturbing the set next to it. Light was reflected inwards from the sides by dull, aluminium-painted reflectors.

Sets were built next to each other when necessary, and since the films were silent, you could be working next door to the Civil War or a boiler works at full blast, while you yourself portrayed a Carmelite nun at prayers. There was no temperament about noise. You just got on with it. Exceptions to this occurred when important stars like the Gishes or Mae Marsh were working. When Sir Herbert Beerbohm Tree came to make *Macbeth* with Constance Collier, John Emerson directing, Sir Herbert asked them to 'take away that black box' (the camera).

Some star directors, like Allan Dwan, were allotted their own units, with a stage used exclusively for their sets and their own studio carpenters, paper-hangers – the works.

Actual film of all unused scenes – anything rejected – was burned in an open incinerator on the back lot, which smelled to high heaven all over the neighbourhood. Film was highly explosive, so they were unable to dispose of it in any other way. They also recovered silver in the burning process.

Mr Griffith told me to acquire some experience before the camera: 'Learn not to get in the way, but stay in the shot. Learn how to make up. Learn professional manners.' So I worked one night in a fire scene on a location near the studio. The set was a modern house exterior which had to be burned down. With the other young girls from the studio I ran around watching the blaze; for this I was given another day's pay, which brought my salary for the week up to five dollars. Usually I carried money as small change tied in the corner of my hankerchief but these dollar bills I carried firmly in my hand.

I could see Mother coming to meet me as I got off the big red Pacific-Electric streetcar, our only means of transport to Hollywood. I held up my hand with fingers spread wide to show how much money I'd received and was annoyed when she didn't kick up her heels with delight. When she reached me I said testily, 'Five dollars.' She said she couldn't believe that was what I'd meant. We were overjoyed – it went to pay the gas or light bill, which were always overdue.

Chapter Three

NOT LONG AFTER I JOINED
Mr Griffith's studio, he said, referring to my good fortune in being
accepted by a company with artistic integrity, I might easily have gone to
a cheap management and been ruined. I opened my eyes very wide and
with a wise nod, said, 'Yes. I know.' (I had heard all about those poor,
ruined girls.) 'Oh!' he snorted. 'I didn't mean *that!*'

As soon as my test was approved, I was put on a guarantee of ten dollars
a week. Immediately afterwards a long-term contract was drawn up
giving me ten dollars a week for the first three months; fifteen dollars for
the next three; twenty dollars for the next six; and so on. The studio didn't
know what they had in me and quite rightly were protecting themselves.
Had many other 'discoveries' been treated in this way, it might have been
far less heartbreaking for them later. Soon this new contract was torn up
and I was given another, for more money – not much, but more.

Although the Triangle Film Corporation was formed at that time, so
that I rode in on the big wave, the studio still made a few two-reelers under
their old banners, either Majestic-Reliance or Mutual. A director of one of
these small films wanted me for an Italian fishing village romance. I tried
on the black wig (my own hair was fair) and the costume, and nearly burst
my hooks and eyes at the thought of being the heroine. Mr Griffith got
wind of it and I was not allowed to do it. 'It's not important enough for
your first film,' I was informed. I didn't believe that for one moment and
wondered why they'd said such a thing.

Triangle had a most enterprising Publicity Department which claimed
a goldmine in my prospects. Anyone Mr Griffith chose to find was news,
and trade papers and magazines had been full of the 'New Find': me. One
day Mr Griffith was talking to a visiting V.I.P. from the press, explaining
the finer points of making films. He told the visitor that I would not be
allowed to appear in a film until the right part came along, although by

now I'd been under contract for a few weeks, maybe months – he turned to me to verify the length of time – and still I had not worked. So the reason why I was whisked out of the Italian fishing village *was* true. I certainly hadn't worked. Anyway, it made a good story. Then one day I was cast to play a Swedish maid in *The Flying Torpedo*.

Since they would have to send a cast list to the press, they now had to make up their minds what they were going to call me. Up till then I'd been called Mary by Mr Griffith because he thought I so resembled his discovery, Miss Pickford, and therefore everyone else did the same. Every person in the studio felt they had a claim on that little lady as they had all worked with her. Even though she had left Griffith for Lasky not long before, they all missed her, and it was a pretty compliment to be dubbed after her. (Miss Pickford once remarked that I resembled her more than her own sister, Lottie, did.)

They said my own name, Juanita Horton, was too long for lights on the front of a theatre and no one east of the Rockies would know how to pronounce it. (Juanita Hansen's name belied their logic: she was by then a famous Mack Sennett beauty.)

In the absence of Mr Griffith, Frank Woods, who had originally greeted me in the studio, renamed me. He was a big man, dressed in grey, an intellectual and a disciplinarian. He had a florid face and wore rimless glasses; he smoked a pipe and took stern command when things went wrong. But when he gave me the name and told me why – before the whole cast – he said it softly and kindly, and I'm sure he meant it. He said, 'Bessie, because any child can pronounce it. And Love, because we want everyone to love her.' Here the unsentimental will squirm. But, uncurl! The reasoning behind the happy-ending film-making of that time was backed up by excellent box-office returns. Without being too cynical, it's a tight argument for making money.

John Emerson had written and was to star in *The Flying Torpedo*, an adaptation from his play *Conspiracy* in which he had also starred as the absent-minded professor. He later married Anita Loos, who was at that time a very young, extremely successful writer on the lot. She looked even smaller than I was and wore her hair in long braids wound round and round her head. She was always laughing whenever I saw her; so were the big shots walking with her and talking to her as an equal. (In London a while back I played the mother of the juvenile lead in a musical of *Gentlemen Prefer Blondes*. Anita Loos flew over to see it, and we had some nostalgic chuckles. You know, when you look into someone's eyes and both of you see the past float by, you don't say much – you don't need to.)

After we'd started rehearsing *The Flying Torpedo*, I met a school friend while waiting down town for a streetcar. She congratulated me on my contract and virtual stardom. But the Italian fishing village with the black wig was still a sore point fresh in my memory. I put her right as to the role I was playing: a maid, and an illiterate, foreign one at that. Not one who would marry the prince in the end. No heroines for me yet.

32

Page One of B.L.'s first album, showing her first part in her first film. From The Flying Torpedo, *made at Griffith's Fine Arts studio, with John Emerson*

I was later told that one of the stars had turned down the part of the little Swede I played. I can see her point. For a schoolgirl to step into the pigeon-toes of a comedy-relief maid was one thing: for an established star to be offered a small role in a story about a bomb that *flies*, of all things, was something else. And the idea of an attack on America by little Japan, who supplied most of our town gardeners, chauffeurs and valets for the whole Pacific coast: absurd!

The film was a gigantic one of its day and necessitated three directors working simultaneously: Jack O'Brien did the dramatic story; Christy Cabanne, one of the studio's top directors, was in charge of the modern armoured battle scenes; and the McCarthy Brothers were responsible for the special effects – miniature sets for destruction, bombs and explosions. Mr Griffith took the last rehearsal as usual, supervising the whole finished work. George Hill – later a big M.G.M. director – was cameraman.

Lucille Young, who played the villainess, gave me some good advice: always put on your own make-up. Never be dependent on a maid for that. Everybody seemed to take it for granted that I was going to become a star – with maids. David Butler, later a well-known actor and then a director for Fox, his father Fred, Raymond Wells and Erich von Stroheim all had small parts in the film. Mr von Stroheim went from Triangle to Universal to do those really grown-up films, so complete to the smallest detail, about the Continent, First World War flavour – *Blind Husbands* and *Foolish Wives*. Lively arguments went on between him and Lucille and the rest of the cast as to what constituted a villain. Mr von Stroheim insisted there was no such thing as an all-evil villain or an all-pure hero; to be real they must be a mixture of both. I wasn't used to hearing such intellectual discussions and to my escape-happy film appreciation this sounded like a foreign dubbing session.

On location for *The Flying Torpedo* one day, we finished only a block or two from where I lived on San Julian Street. I was too shy to ask them to drop me off home and went back with the unit clear across Los Angeles to Hollywood, changed clothes and took a streetcar straight back to almost the same spot I'd left a couple of hours before. When the unit discovered this they thought I was bats. But I hadn't known whether they would be allowed to go a block out of their way to take me home. Also, I'd left all my clothes at the studio and the idea of having to get together another outfit of my own for next morning might have contributed to my reticence. The costume I wore for the film, which is now in the National Film Archive, consisted of a grey flannel peasant dress with tight bodice and full skirt; tight jacket with wide revers; black and white horizontal-striped stockings and oversized black and white flat co-respondent shoes with two straps and buttons, one missing. I didn't fancy riding on a streetcar next morning dressed like that.

In about 1930 I was in *Conspiracy* for R.K.O., Mr Cabanne directing and Ned Sparks playing the absent-minded professor. I took some time to realize it was the original *Flying Torpedo* which I knew only by its film name. This time I was the leading lady – and there was no Swedish maid.

Intolerance, which they had been making when I first set foot on the Griffith lot – and they were still at it when I was doing *The Flying Torpedo* – concerned four stretches of history: the Babylonian period, the Biblical time of Jesus, the persecution of the French Huguenots and the modern period of wealth and poverty in America. They were told simultaneously, cutting from one to another.

I played the Bride of Cana in the Biblical period. George Walsh, brother of the director Raoul Walsh, was the Bridegroom. Between scenes on our bridal dais he taught me a Fordham University song or yell to be sung to the traditional Jewish wedding song:

Oi! Oi! Oi! Oi! Mazeltov! Mazeltov!
Rosh Hashana! Rosh Hashana!
Yom Kippur! Yom Kippur!
Fordham! Fordham!
Team! Team! Team! Team! Team!

The marriage at Cana in D. W. Griffith's Intolerance. *B.L. and George Walsh as the bride and groom, right, being blessed by Christ Jesus (Howard Gaye)*

For our wedding scene, scores and scores of Orthodox Jews from Temple Street in town were used as crowd artistes. At noon they were tactlessly served a box lunch with ham in it. This particular day I didn't feel well and was sent home, which was not far, but as I was scantily clad, with bare feet and dancing bells, Mother and I were taken in a car. The Wise Old Men on the wedding set looked wiser than ever and nodded solemnly to each other, their hands tucked into their sleeves: it was the ham!

Rabbi Myers, father of my school friends Carmel and Zion, was technical adviser on the Biblical period. He once told us how it pained him to go into a great library: he acted out how it crushed his head to see the number of precious books, knowing he would never be able to read them all. His name for automobiles: Messengers of Death. Some time later I was with the family party and waiting for him to join us when we heard the news that he had been killed by a car on the Edendale Viaduct.

Many Griffith actors and assistant directors were capable of taking out a second unit for 'chases' (cars, horses or people chasing or being chased), or for directing crowd scenes, battle scenes or the like. In *Intolerance*, half a dozen of them were made up, in costume and mingled in shot with the

D. W. Griffith, with a megaphone, directs an exterior shot from Intolerance

crowds, inciting the mob and relaying the directions of Mr Griffith, who stood on a high platform, calmly shouting through a megaphone. I can still see George Siegmann, who played Cyrus in the Babylonian period, disguised in a loose shift and girdle, a scarf over his head and shoulders held in place by a circlet over his forehead, and I can still hear his great booming voice. Then there was dear, quiet Tom Wilson bellowing away too, whose actress-dancer wife, Grace, was one of the dancers at Belshazzar's Feast.

Among the other actor-cum-assistants who became directors were Elmer Clifton and Joseph Henabery. Elmer played the Rhapsode in the Babylonian period; one day he was to be my leading man in *Acquitted* and *Nina The Flower Girl*, and later still was to make *Down To The Sea In Ships*, which discovered Clara Bow. Joseph Henabery had played Abraham Lincoln in *The Birth Of A Nation*. He looked just like the pictures of Lincoln, and, so it was said, thought like him. Ten years later he directed me in *Tongues Of Flame* for Lasky's, in New York.

Not all of these stalwarts became stars or directors; but they were the solid foundation of the Griffith spectacle. Without their unlimited energy and devotion to their jobs, the huge crowd scenes could never have had such authority. Nor was their job made easier by extra slackers who would hide behind the set, go to sleep or get out of shot to play cards. They had to be routed out and made to go back to work – that hasn't changed.

One day during the filming of the Biblical period of *Intolerance*, Lillian Gish was watching the frenzied scene of Christ Jesus surrounded by an angry mob as he carries his Cross along a narrow, winding street. The camera had to move back before the on-surging mob and the Cross in a tracking shot, a new technique. As it moved back, shooting down on the crowd, the heavy squared posts laid across to smooth the way for the camera dolly had to be pulled out of shot on each side. Mr Griffith, directing the scene through his megaphone, was standing beside his cameraman Billy Bitzer, with Lillian on the other side. When the scene reached its pitch, everyone hysterical, yelling, wild-eyed, spitting, cursing, tearing each others' clothes off, quite out of control and screaming: 'Crucify him! Cru-u-ucify him!', Lillian burst into tears – in spite of all the technical trappings – and, almost hysterical herself, had to leave.

I wish there was more of this in crowd scenes now: more attention paid to detail, more human emotion shown by every actor in the crowds. Today you never see conviction on their faces, let alone in their movements. Nobody is hilariously glad, murderously angry or desolately sad any more. A lot of people just say 'Ah', as they would for the doctor, when they are supposed to be watching someone being hanged, drawn and quartered.

Howard Gaye had the part of Christ Jesus in the Biblical period. During that shooting, Howard stopped smoking and went teetotal – he felt it would be sacrilegious to do otherwise. But you should have heard De Wolf Hopper's colourful story of coming on to the Wedding at Cana and suddenly seeing Howard – with blonde beard, sandals and flowing robes – stepping out of a Ford.

The last time I saw *Intolerance* I was struck by the extraordinary beauty of the Griffith girls. Beauty of even your dearest friends, when you sit next to it every day and discuss what you had for breakfast, gets taken for granted. In the Temple of Ishtar scene alone, the screen was choc-a-bloc with breath-taking beauties: Pauline Starke, Mildred Harris (the future Mrs Charles Chaplin), Winifred Westover (the future Mrs William S. Hart), Carmel Myers, Seena Owen and many others.

Top female stars at the studio were the Gishes, Lillian and Dorothy, and Mae Marsh. Two of Mae's three sisters, her brother and her brother-in-law were all working at the Griffith studio. (I cried myself to sleep one night because Mr Griffith had told me I would never be as good an actress as Mae Marsh. Maybe I'd been getting a little out of hand – or, of course, it just might have been true.) Of the men, Bobby Harron was always the young lead; Wilfred Lucas and Henry Walthall were among the older ones.

Other film stars on the lot at the same time were Miriam Cooper, Teddy Sampson and Fay Tincher. Norma Talmadge, famous for years with Vitagraph, joined us, as well as Constance and another sister, Natalie (future Mrs Buster Keaton). Then there were the New York and London stars: Sir Herbert Beerbohm Tree and Constance Collier, John

Stars at Griffith's
Fine Arts studio,
February, 1916.
Back row, from left:
Dorothy Gish,
Seena Owen,
Norma Talmadge;
centre row:
Bobby Harron,
Harry Aitken,
Sir Herbert Beerbohm Tree,
Owen Moore,
Wilfred Lucas;
front row:
Douglas Fairbanks Sr,
B.L.,
Constance Talmadge,
Constance Collier,
Lillian Gish,
Fay Tincher,
De Wolf Hopper

Emerson, Marie Doro, De Wolf Hopper and Douglas Fairbanks. Mrs Fairbanks, former Beth Sully, was her husband's business manager and they brought their son, Douglas Junior, and his governess. That lady was furious when Senior let Junior in among his make-up and he came out painted as white as a sheet.

With De Wolf Hopper was his actress wife, Hedda – later *the* Hedda Hopper, gossip writer with the screwy hats. De Wolf Hopper was a great *raconteur* and delighted in relating his first film experiences: 'Dying one afternoon and not even shot until three weeks later! *Fas*-cin-a-ting!' He made one picture, with Fay Tincher, about a lion which breaks loose and roams around the hotel where he is trying to book a room. The big lobby set was on one of the open stages and was fenced off with heavy metal mesh and cages at every entrance. Even the cameras were in cages. Only the keeper ever came on the set with the lion, and everybody watched from a judicious distance. Mr Griffith was once showing the Governor of California round while shooting was going on. Suddenly he left the Governor and walked on to the set with the lion. Very quietly Mr Stillman – that really was the photographer's name – took some stills with his tripod camera. And then, I'm very glad to say, Mr Griffith walked out again, followed by Mr Stillman with his cumbersome Kodak.

Everyone on the lot worked together in those days. I once saw the studio street-cleaner make a suggestion to Mr Griffith as he watched him directing Mae Marsh in a scene for the Modern period of *Intolerance*. It doesn't necessarily follow that the idea was used, but Mr Griffith listened.

The studio was always teeming with people. Small-part players were probably only on a guarantee, paid more when they worked more, but they all came to the studio every day except the stars. Many of these people were there when I arrived, dating even from Biograph days. So many were as patient and kind to me as the saints.

Dozens of husbands and wives, sometimes whole families, worked there. The Browns, for instance: Mrs Lucille Brown was an actress as well as studio matron and chaperone; Mr Brown was an actor; and young Karl Brown, their son, was assistant to Billy Bitzer, Mr Griffith's cameraman. Karl was a studious young man: I never saw him smile. He was always making tests of some kind on his own, either concerning his camera or *Intolerance*. One was of Pauline Starke in a Babylonian dancing girl's costume, wearing a leopard's head. I was supposed to be used for that experiment, too, but I had the presence of mind to be rehearsing at the time.

There was a studio dog. He was fawn-coloured, sleek-haired, long-nosed, and his name was Props. He came and went as he pleased, and for meals would go home with Lloyd Ingraham or any of the directors, assistants or prop men from the old Biograph. Mr Ingraham would sometimes wrap a handkerchief round one of Props's forefeet and say, 'Poor Props! Poor Props!' Props would look up mournfully and limp around feeling sorry for himself until he was 'healed' by having his bandage removed. He was a veteran of the screen: I even saw him once as a puppy in an old Biograph film.

We sometimes rehearsed for *Intolerance* upstairs in the extra men's dressing-room, a big, new, unpainted frame building. I always remember how to pronounce the name of the god Baal from the time we were rehearsing the Babylonian period there. The dressing-room was very cold and Mr Griffith, in his stentorian voice, rhymed, 'The priests of Baal are cold as hell.'

I once saw Mildred Harris in that same rehearsal room, standing in a shaft of light coming from a small window high up in the wall behind her and to her left. Mildred was so tenderly beautiful, so young, just growing up: her hair, which was blonde and naturally curly, fell over her shoulders and the light gave her a halo. Mr Griffith caught sight of her: 'Mildred,' he said, 'don't move. You must always find a light and look like that.'

Mr Griffith still called me Mary – he never did call me anything else – so when we were on the indoor stage another time rehearsing and Mr Griffith suddenly bellowed 'Mary!', everybody on the lot knew that meant me. Like Mildred, without realizing it, I was standing in the light, wearing a thin white dress; but *I* was wearing school bloomers underneath. 'Mary!' he repeated sharply, 'Get out of the light!'

I was never shy with Mr Griffith, even from the beginning. I'm sure I could have taken any problem to him; he inspired confidence in everyone. Once – it must have been between set-ups during the filming of *Intolerance* – we were talking. It was extraordinary: I'd only been on the lot a few weeks, and he knew nothing about my childhood, yet he told me my whole life story. He read me like a book. He told me about my mother, my father, our hardships – heartaches – ambitions — disappointments – practically from the time I was born! I was soon drenched with my own tears – and I never did cry much in a studio, I waited till I got home.

Mr Griffith could understand the inner workings of people. Understanding, compassion, interest in others: that's what it takes and that's what he had. He was a good director, and he was also a great man.

B. L. at the bungalow on Fountain Avenue, with ukelele

Chapter Four

AT LAST CAME THE BIG DAY, THE final step, no going back, and we moved to Hollywood. It was thirty-six blocks from our San Julian Street home to the middle of town, and another forty-five blocks from the middle of town going west. Eighty-one blocks divided by twelve gives you six and three-quarter miles. That's not far as the crows fly out home, but psychologically it was moon-walking. And on entering that magical world of Art, those precious precincts forbidden to all except the chosen few; on experiencing the unimagined bliss of owning more than one pair of shoes; on having the sacred right to set foot on those streets (which got muddy when it rained) . . . what impressed me most about the place? What seemed absolutely incredible about Hollywood? The soft water. Yes, sir, it was just like pure rainwater. It came from a different source from Los Angeles' supply and it stayed that way until they mucked it up with the Owens River project – diverting a whole river over our way. Oh, it was perfectly clean and there was nothing wrong with it. It opened up a million or so acres of desert land for farming, and now they can't carry away all the stuff that grows there, but it was *hard* water with salts and things. So soon, like everyone else, we too had the familiar rack and up-ended bottle from Arrowhead Springs on our back porch.

We rented a new bungalow on Fountain Avenue, directly across from the back lot of the studio. Our landlord, Mr McIntosh, and his family, had the house next door, on the corner. The McIntoshes had three children: Raymond and Harold, maybe sixteen and fourteen, and Marjorie, a bit younger. They must have come from the country, as they were just like our family. At night, after dinner, the boys would take their two bicycles and their sister and me, the two of us riding on the cross-bars, and we would go for miles. After Dad had got a car – a little Maxwell for which I paid, although I said I wouldn't because it was bought without telling me – we were for ever driving to places I'd already been to with the McIntosh children and their wheels.

Another new pastime for me on Fountain Avenue was looking after a dozen finest Plymouth Rock chickens. We built a high wire fence for them and I used to sit beside it and talk or sing to them. They would come over to the wire netting and croon back to me. When we moved again and disposed of them, I felt like a criminal. I had let them down – my closest friends!

Perhaps the night after a bicycle ride I would go to an opening of one of the films made on the lot, escorted by a big-wig film exhibitor from the Middle West. Many of these important people became friends and I would meet their wives and families when they accompanied them (the *very* next time they came to California), or when I went through their territory on location or to open a new theatre. For social functions I was always chaperoned by Marion Strauch from Publicity. She saw that everything was done in style – orchids, chauffeured limousine, the lot.

I would be wearing a dinner dress with demure cap sleeves – no naked shoulders. Besides being in good taste, that was the Griffith formula for a young girl. The first dress Mother and I bought for me, to be worn at night, was purchased at J. W. Robinson's, an excellent department store with a French Room on 7th Street. We were wise enough to ask a friend along: we knew Mrs Gibson would have good taste and know where to buy things. I must admit that I was disappointed with the pale pink georgette crêpe and tiny black velvet bow. I had been hoping for a little number slashed to the waist, back and front. Mrs Gibson said as they were wrapping it up that she was so glad to see me choose something modest. She felt the modern trend of young girls showing neck and arms very bold. I sighed. It was the sigh of the lonely rich.

The studio had their hands full making a lady of me. As far as the young girls were concerned – there were no young boys – our behaviour was governed by the invisible reins of a charm school. There was so much to learn . . . Mr Griffith wanted me to develop poise, proper posture, to walk not run – in fact, to have stage training. So I joined the girls for body movement whenever they rehearsed in the studio, and took singing lessons from Constantino, a Spanish tenor and singing teacher, to develop my chest – bust, I suppose.

Mr Constantino looked like all Latin singers when they reach about forty. He wore a wide-brimmed, floppy black hat as befitted his role. He had sung with Tetrazzini when she made her debut at the Metropolitan Opera House in 1911, and used to tell me anecdotes about her. He lived in a prosperous residential neighbourhood, in a solid frame house with a big front porch on the east side of a palm-lined street. He gave lessons in his sitting-room, on one wall of which was a painting of Nydia, the Blind Girl, a character in Bulwer Lytton's *Last Days Of Pompeii*. I believe this picture was the inspiration for Mother when she wrote her scenario, *Nina The Flower Girl*, which was later made at the Griffith studio with me in the name part.

My first lesson in theatrical etiquette: Mr Frank Woods told my mother never to allow me to use the word 'Movies'. Motion Pictures or Moving Pictures were the correct phrases. 'Movies' could not have been more vulgar if spelt with four letters – and *chaperoned* was writ in large capitals.

Mrs Lucille Brown, as matron, was in charge of all the girls and women. Away from the studio, people did as they pleased (and that statement lacks imagination); on the lot, Mrs Brown's word was law. She was a small blonde dragon with a purposeful walk who always wore a hat with a feather or flower sticking up. No male, by whatever urgent excuse or plausible accident, could have invaded any part of the women's dressing-rooms. With her around, your daughter was as safe and well mannered as in a convent.

Meanwhile my mother had given up her job and was now with me the whole time I was in the studios until I had personal maids who were never out of reach. Since she was always with me, it was only natural that she should be dubbed with my name, becoming Mrs Love. Marion Strauch from Publicity, in whom the whole family had gained a good friend, had started it. She was like another daughter to my mother and was soon calling her 'Mother Love'. I wonder what Dad thought of it. He was so proud of me going into films, I don't think changing *my* name would have bothered him. Using both names as one came easy to my parents as Southerners do that anyway – Bessie-Love is what they called me, and people who knew us then still do. However, Mrs Love is quite another thing, and I once heard someone address Dad as Doctor Love!

But by then, the day-to-day, or minute-to-minute, business at hand was so completely different from anything we had ever experienced in our lives, that changing one's name today and address tomorrow was all part of it – and the one was no more important than the other.

Stars of our studio did not appear in public, opening fêtes and so on. For some reason I was given this to do – perhaps to get used to meeting people and the press, to create an image and knock some of the angles into curves. Before my first press interview I asked Mr Griffith what I should say. He said, 'Just tell the truth.' I think that approach has stayed with me and I always expect each encounter to be a friendly one.

The first time I received a fan letter I was going to return it. Since the person was unknown to me I thought it was a mistake. Mr Griffith explained what a fan and a fan letter were, that I would receive many in due course, and that I was never to answer them personally, nor send a photograph on the first request. (I must have tried going broke early on with those photographs. I supplied ten by eight inch sepias on pebble paper. Eventually we got smart and ordered repros, first by hundreds, then thousands, then ten thousand.) I was taught not to speak to strangers on the telephone, and the number was non-listed – it still is.

Maud Adams was always the example held up to us. On tour she lived in her own private railroad car which was hooked up to the train when it was time to move on, and she was never seen outside the theatre. It's understandable that people don't want to spend hard-earned money to see you in *The Duchess Of Malfi* at the matinée and then run into you with your hair in curlers buying a hot dog for supper. That's not being snobbish, it just makes sense. There are other reasons for never being seen off duty. Actors are just human beings and people don't like to find that out. Mr Griffith warned me: 'Never meet your film favourites! You'll be disappointed.'

With the Hollywood jump came not so much a social life – that would imply other people were involved – but whereas before we'd gone to the

46

Orpheum on Saturday nights, now we didn't have to wait until the weekend. While I was at Griffith's the family went to see all the films made by the studio – and we didn't miss the good ones made elsewhere. But the Orpheum was still the star attraction. Except for film nights, or when I had to work late at the studio, we went to the theatre every night.

Like all good vaudeville houses in their hey-hey day, the Orpheum had excellent bills starring world-famous celebrities. Some of the head-liners were Lillian Russell; Gertrude Hoffman with her dancing troupe; Sophie Tucker; Blossom Seely; the much-married Nat Goodwin; (Poker Game) Bert Williams; The Two Black Crows; Dancing Bill Robinson – later, when I was doing the Charleston 'at the slightest provocation', as Eddie Sutherland said, Bill Robinson did an impression of me in his act. I was dying to see it, but the night I went he (probably tactfully) refrained.

Many of the celebrities who played at the Orpheum went into films. Some of them I was to work with later. I made my first Talking Picture with the littlest Foy of Eddie Foy and The Seven Little Foys, Eddie Junior, who became my beau. He told me he'd once skipped a performance of their act to see his idol William S. Hart in *The Aryan* (my second film, not counting *Intolerance*). Harry Langdon had a hilarious automobile act at the Orpheum. Later I did *See America Thirst*, a comedy about prohibition, with him and Slim Summerville, again after sound came in . . .

El Brendel, of Swedish – born in Philadelphia – origin, progressed from the Orpheum to Fox Studios. His speciality for the finish of his act consisted of his entire suit falling apart at the seams. Then there was old-timer Bill Demarest, with his 'cello-playing. He would fall flat on his back after failing some gymnastic attempt, then quietly resume his 'cello-playing. After a brief musical rendering he would take up the gymnastics again, with the same result. That's all his act consisted of; the gag was repeated over and over, you knew what he was going to do, and yet you waited for it with tears running down your face. What a beautiful comic. Like many another, he came to Hollywood via the Orpheum, and stayed.

So now we lived in Hollywood. We'd changed address, yes, but then we were always changing our address; and I would not be going down town to high school any more, instead I would go across the street to the studio every day. And about owning that 'other pair' of shoes I spoke of earlier – my chum from L.A. High School, Floren Levitt, came over one day for a visit. (We were old friends from McKinley Grammar School for a start, and when I had turned up on my first day at L.A. High, forlorn and alone, Floren had taken me under the shelter of her small wing and stayed back in my classroom, Number 35, with me rather than go up with her own class.) Literally within the same year as my move to Hollywood, she and I had been going down one of the many corridors at school when I caught the worn sole of my left shoe on a thin slab of splinter in the floor. It never touched my foot, but ran the full length inside my slipper before breaking off. We both got the giggles and had great difficulty in sobering up to go on to Latin and political economy. Now, in Fountain Avenue and giggling again, I led Floren to my present shoe cupboard, which held more than a couple of dozen pairs. We fell about, she and I, at the sight of all those shoes – everything you could think of except moccasins.

Though we may not have realized it, Floren and I knew lots of people in pictures who'd gone to L.A. with us. There was Carmel Myers and her brother Zion; Marie Prevost's chic sister Marjorie (who couldn't be chic with such a sister to get your clothes from?); Morris Ankrum – Shakespearean actor, no less; Nate Dychess and Harry Brand, who ran the publicity offices of various studios; Bob Lander, a prop man at First National and the son of the restaurant owner Mother had worked for. One day on the lot Bob, who never had smiled when I was little, grabbed me, hugged me and threw me up in the air, shouting, 'I've got it! Hooray!' I think he'd probably got a promotion and a rise by the sound of it. Lonnie Dorsey, now working at Mack Sennett's, used to carry my books at McKinley. One day on the way home he'd said, 'I've been kicked out of every school I've ever attended but what are *you* doing at McKinley?' Even dear little De Witt Saunders had lived with us while a patient of Dad's – we adored him. When he grew to be a big De Witt he was a stage hand in the down-town Pantages Theatre while I was doing the Fanchon & Marco touring revue. So lots of people in pictures had the same background as mine – and those who didn't were just other people.

And the future? I was far too busy keeping up with the present to think about that. I wasn't going to be a teacher, and that's for sure. Anyway, if you did think about it at all, you just saw it going on and on, getting better and better. I had a contract proving it would. And working in the best studio in the world for the best man in the world – well, it would just go on and on.

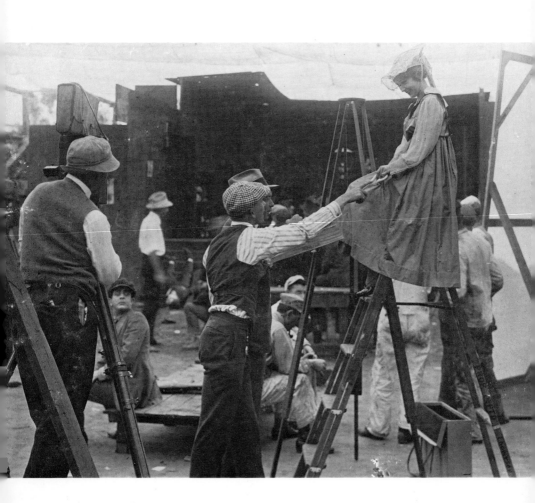

Chapter Five

TRIANGLE FILM CORPORATION consisted of three separate film production companies headed by D. W. Griffith, Thos. H. Ince and Mack Sennett respectively. That is not to say they were under one roof. They were miles apart. Mr Griffith's Fine Arts studio was in Hollywood; Mr Ince was at Inceville, about fifteen miles west to the ocean and then more miles up the coast; and Sennett's Keystone Comedies studio was in Edendale, five or ten miles east of Hollywood.

I was on the Keystone lot only once, when our Publicity Department took Mother and me. I met a young slapstick comic, Bobby Vernon, and Harry McCoy, a star comic and composer of best-selling rag-time tunes, 'Oceana Roll' among them. I was fascinated by all the props, people, explosions and door slammings. Ford Sterling was playing his usual Chief-of-Police, yelling in deep guttural German accent: 'Station h-h-h-house!', pointing to the door and looking into the camera to bellow, 'Get h-h-h-hout!' Fifteen years later, when Ford had turned straight actor, he and I worked together at M.G.M. in *The Girl In The Show*, from the play *Eva The Fifth*.

I was loaned by Mr Griffith to Thomas H. Ince for the second film I made, *The Aryan*, starring William S. Hart. Mr Hart had wanted either Mae Marsh or one of the Gishes for his next leading lady. Mr Griffith paid me the compliment of offering my services instead. While this might have been a polite way of saying 'No', since our studio was full of pretty girls and clever young actresses, I was accepted anyway.

Surrounding the Ince studio, all the way back into the mountains from the ocean, was harsh country which served as locations for China, the Scottish Highlands or any other remote, craggy place that happened to crop up in the script. (Now the coastline is solid with houses and beach clubs.) The buildings at Inceville were low and rambling bungalow-type

Inceville, at the foot of the Santa Monica mountains

buildings, as were all the other studios then, but Ince's were unique in that they were built to be used as exterior sets. Cutting-rooms, dressing-rooms or offices would be found in a Scottish Fishing Village, a Far Western Town, or perhaps something Ye Olde. If you were a cutter and your lunch break came while someone was 'dying' right outside your woolly-West front door, you would just have to wait for your snack until he was truly 'dead' and the director yelled, 'Cut!'

Within two years – I could never have guessed – that studio had moved to Culver City and I was under contract there. Later the studio's name was changed to Goldwyn, when it was owned by Sam Goldfish and Edgar Selwyn and then by Sam Goldfish (who changed his name to Goldwyn) alone. Still later it became Metro-Goldwyn-Mayer.

They did work with a script at Ince's – a thick one. They didn't rehearse the play as a whole before starting to shoot, as we did with Mr Griffith, but only before each scene, as everyone else did and still does. Nonetheless you were supposed to be word-perfect at Ince's. C. Gardner Sullivan wrote *The Aryan* and the lines were to be spoken as written, no matter how long the speeches and despite the fact that only the beginning and end would be used, the middle bit coming to rest on the cutting-room floor.

Meeting the ferocious Mr Hart and his villainous gang in The Aryan

The contents of the middle bit would appear in the printed sub-titles on the screen; at Ince's these were sometimes amusingly illustrated.

The expression 'rushes' – film from the previous day's work, run through in the studio – comes from Inceville. It took some time to have the completed film finally developed in the one big Rothacker-Aller laboratory for distribution to the theatres. But daily work was rushed through our own studio laboratories, developed and dried on great revolving drums (cylinders made up of slats running lengthways). You could then see the results in the projection room after the next day's shooting and check for re-takes.

Another expression, 'Get friendly', meaning 'Come closer to the camera', was first used by Joe August, Mr Hart's cameraman, and was taken up by the whole company.

Alice Taafe, who changed her name to Alice Terry, was one of the small part players at Inceville. She married Rex Ingram and starred in his beautiful films made out home and in France – *The Four Horsemen* and *Mare Nostrum* among them. Jack Gilbert – known to the public as John – was then also a small-part player. He doubled – even trebled – in *The Aryan*, first as an Indian, then as a frontiersman, and finally as one of Mr Hart's blood-curdling wild brood. Jack would one day be my leading man in *Dawn Of Understanding*, and later still I would be his leading lady in *St Elmo* for Fox.

The Ince stars furnished their own rooms from scratch – for in this as in other respects Tom Ince was not noted for his generosity in the studio. Joseph Dowling, a fine old actor, was talking about him one day: 'What can you do with Ince?' he said. 'You go to his office, saying to yourself, "I've had enough of the way I'm being paid. This is iniquitous." You knock on the door, you go inside. And you come out on your hands and knees. You not only don't get a rise, but your salary's been cut! What can you do with him?'

Mr Hart used to collect my mother and me every morning. I cannot think how we would have got to Inceville otherwise. The location for *The Aryan* was the sand dunes south of Playa del Rey, miles south of Santa Monica. At that time it was literally nothing but sand dunes and the only transport was a rickety streetcar, open all around, with seats athwart it, which lazily bucked and wobbled as it progressed. The extras made their way to work under their own steam – some may have got lifts, some came on that streetcar – and they brought their own lunches. (At Griffith's we went to location in a Cadillac, a Pierce-Arrow, a Packard and such, with drivers; and we ate at good, middle-class restaurants.)

I worshipped Mr Hart almost as much as I did Mr Griffith. He was an important star in the new, grander film world. He co-directed his films with Cliff Smith, and wrote some of his own stories; he told me that he was writing by dictation during the lunch hour in his dressing-room. He was idolized by his fans all over the world, as was his horse. (The horse's screen name was Paint, or Pinto, which is Spanish for the same thing, but his real name was Fritz. He received fan mail, too.)

In *The Aryan*, as in many of his other films, Mr Hart played a big bad man with a heart of gold. We arrived at the scene where I – simple, artless Mary Jane of the wagon train – was to meet the cut-throat leader of a lawless community, Mr Hart. Innocent trust in the inherent goodness of any white man – regardless of what anybody else had seen or suffered – was the key to the little lady's character, and the key-note of the film, hence the title, *The Aryan*. As you may have guessed, this attitude reformed him.

The day we came to take this scene, my beloved Mr Hart must have wafted my mother and me to the studio as usual. And Joe August must have exercised his usual skill in lighting the scene. We must have rehearsed it many times, and everybody, including me, would have known exactly what was to happen. The cameras turned; Mr Hart put on that savage, maniacal expression he wore as a villain and bellowed at me like Leo the M.G.M. lion; and I went straight under the table.

Everybody came to my rescue, including Mr Hart, explaining that he didn't *really* mean it; it was only a play and he was still my friend. In the scene I was not supposed to be frightened. I tried in my turn to reassure them that I did understand perfectly and I was not a scrap afraid. I calmed down. We did it again. From looking like St John himself, Mr Hart let out one snarl and this time I shot up the wall . . . I don't know how long we kept at it, but the film was a great success so the point must have been made: I was not afraid!

By 1915 such epics as *Cabiria* and *Quo Vadis* had already been made in Italy, and France had had for years a most sophisticated film industry, especially in trick photography, not to mention their slapstick comedies with the great Max Linder. They were even bold enough in the very early days to have a young woman director, Mlle Alice Guy – who in 1917, as Alice Guy-Blaché, would direct a film of mine for Pathé in New York. That was *Spring Of The Year*, also called *The Great Adventure*.

But meantime with the First World War the picture business in Europe was *kaput*. This gave Hollywood an edge on production, and it was years before we faced serious competition again from abroad.

The newly-formed Triangle Film Corporation was a pioneer in presenting a weekly change of good films in the grand manner. Its Los Angeles opening was a gala occasion at Clune's Auditorium. Each of the three studios – Griffith, Ince, Sennett – showed a film. Ours was *The Lamb*, Fairbanks' first. Sennett's Keystone Comedies presented *My Valet*, a rather grand slapstick affair with Mabel Normand and two big New York comedians, Willie Collier and Raymond Hitchcock; and Ince showed *The Iron Strain*, directed by Reginald Barker and starring Dustin Farnum, Enid Markey and Louise Glaum.

I was in Mr Hart's party, sitting next to him. In one film there was a scene where a group of circus 'statues' backstage were getting ready to pose for one of those tableaux, surrounded by a very thick, very black velvet curtain, which is hauled up to reveal 'The Death of Cleopatra' or the like. The statues, to look like marble, were wearing white skin-tights. You should have heard the gasps from that American audience. Mr Hart expressed himself very frankly in loud stage-whispered disbelief. Actually, the statues did nothing shocking. It was just that we were unused to seeing them without orthodox clothing on the orthodox places. Things are different now.

Having finished work with Mr Hart at Inceville, I returned to my home studio. They were still making *Intolerance*. This was Thanksgiving time, the end of November; I had had my audition during rehearsals of the Babylonian period five months previously, at the end of June.

Soon I was cast in *Acquitted*, with Wilfred Lucas playing my father, Carmen de Rue my little sister, Mary Alden my mother, and Elmer Clifton as leading man. Paul Powell directed this and many other films I was in subsequently. We worked on location at the Bishop family home, the candy people. Few things seem to have bowled me over then, but this was one of them. For one thing, I knew the name Bishop from the candy –

which made it seem like working in a fairy-tale house. It was also the first really beautiful home I'd ever seen the inside of.

On the Griffith lot my work, or that of any leading lady, usually took two to four weeks per film. The complete film took longer, unlike the ones made by cheap studios. At ours, any scene which needed to be added or re-taken after a look at the first cut could be done, since all the actors were under long contracts and were therefore available, even though working on another film by then. As my work began to snowball, I did this a lot.

Two weeks after *Acquitted* had been finished, Mr Griffith gave a luncheon for everybody rehearsing in *Intolerance*. That meant the entire studio. The party was held upstairs in the extra men's big dressing-room where I'd seen Mildred Harris and her halo, and the food and serving staff were imported from the Alexandria Hotel, Los Angeles, twenty miles away. There was nothing comparable in Hollywood at the time; champagne flowed and our film feast of Belshazzar was hardly more elegant. This was no box lunch.

That same afternoon Benny Zeidman, head of Publicity, took me in a studio car to the *Los Angeles Tribune* office for my first press interview. Next night *The Flying Torpedo*, by no means an *Intolerance*, but spectacular enough in its war scenes, had its première at the Burbank Theatre down town. This was no hole-in-the-wall nickelodeon but the same Burbank where I had gone as a child on 'comps' to see live theatre. And it, my first film, initiated the Burbank as a 'picture show'. I was taken down front and given a bouquet, and people crowded round us until we had difficulty leaving. Mother wrote in her diary, 'Babe made her official bow to the public'. In spite of this, a couple of weeks later we did yet another scene for *The Flying Torpedo*!

Very soon I was chosen as Douglas Fairbanks' leading lady in *The Good Bad Man*, his second film and first western. I wanted to jump over the moon and was rushing off to tell him so when my informant said, 'Thank *Mrs* Fairbanks. She's the one who chose you.'

We had a whole house with a big bare yard to rehearse in. I was given a revolver with some blanks in order to get used to firing the thing. I lacked discretion as to how much, how often and at whom to fire, and my target practice soon caused all arms to be recalled.

Even on the stage in New York before he entered films, Douglas Fairbanks was the athletic, smiling, typical all-American hero. He played polo and all the gentlemanly sports and could learn to do anything, including trick riding and spinning a rope. Eventually he had his own fully-equipped gymnasium and a trainer in his own studio.

Fairbanks brought a new quirk to melodramatic situations. They were always sent up, always played for laughs. Even when the crooks were thrown over cliffs, sprung in their own traps or bobbing at the end of a rope, it was funny, with him rescuing The Girl in some spectacular way. He never had a double, taking pride in doing the stunts himself. And it

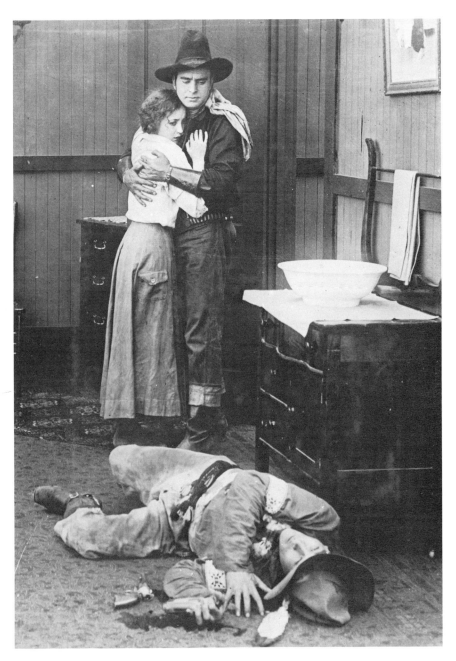

Fairbanks protecting B.L. in The Good Bad Man, *Charlie Stevens lying dead on the floor*

was pretty frustrating for him when an audience took the use of doubles for granted. It was easy for him to make a quick getaway from the bandits by a running jump from the ground, landing on the horse's rump, bouncing into the saddle and off to the hills. To rescue me from the outlaws in *The Good Bad Man* he came riding up at full tilt, hoicked me up behind him and galloped back the way he'd come. I had no double for that either, but there's not much credit due. The rider in that stunt does all the work; the one hoicked has nothing to do but be exactly where she's supposed to be, and willing.

He was of beautiful build, lithe as a leopard – but not tall. And no one can go on for ever digging holes for his leading lady to stand in, or hanging from a chandelier to make love to her, even if it is Signe Auen or Julanne Johnston with all her supple Ali Baba beauty. My height was – and is – five feet. For some reason I've always photographed taller than I am. So next to me Mr Fairbanks looked six foot tall. At one time he had in mind making me his permanent leading lady; we would make a film team like others on stage and screen.

Mr Fairbanks was always enthusiastic about some project for the future, pinning his all on it. I said I'd be afraid to do that in case it failed. 'No! No!' he exclaimed (he always talked in exclamation marks). 'What does it matter! In that case you pin your hopes to something else!'

He used to tell me how modest Charlie Chaplin, Mary Pickford and the other big stars were. He was extremely kind. He told me to observe cultured people, how they talked, walked, conducted themselves – not to copy them, just to learn how the other half lived.

Mr Fairbanks' cameraman was Victor Fleming, who became a director (ten years later I worked with him at the Lasky studios in *Son Of His Father* by Zane Grey). When Vic and Mr Fairbanks were travelling on the Santa Fé Express one time, they had a bet to see which of them could go from their compartment and drawing-room to the dining-car without touching the floor. So they 'walked' through the coaches, hanging on to anything overhead and clinging to the seats, which faced each other. History does not record the winner – or the other passengers' reactions.

The second film I made with Fairbanks was *Reggie Mixes In*, directed by Christy Cabanne. There's a good, well-planned rough-and-tumble fight in it, when Reggie surprises everybody by mixing in to rescue the leading lady (me) from thugs in a cheap dance-hall. Nothing was ever accidentally good about Fairbanks' work. Everything was carefully planned.

The third I did with him was a two-reeler, *The Mystery Of The Leaping Fish* (we called it The Leaping Tuna). It was a send-up of Sherlock Holmes – checked suit, deer-stalker, false moustache *et al.* – which didn't quite come off. As I've said, Mr Fairbanks was a perfectionist: 'I can't seem to get the right *voice* for this character!' he would say in his quick, breathy way – in spite of the fact that it was a silent film.

The story: a foreign narcotics ring and their beautiful accomplice Alma Rubens smuggle dope into the country hidden in beach-play equipment.

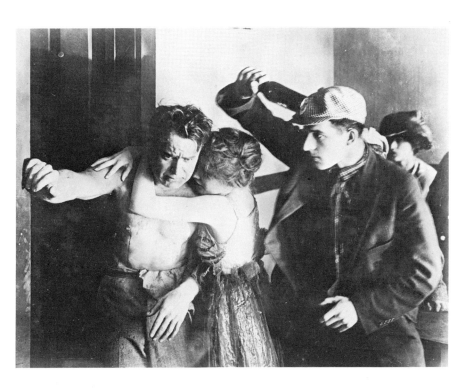

Above: *The great dance-hall fight in* Reggie Mixes In. *B.L., Fairbanks and Frank Bennett brandishing the bottle.* Right: The Mystery Of The Leaping Fish: *B.L. tied up for her kidnapping scene which caused a real-life fight in Chinatown*

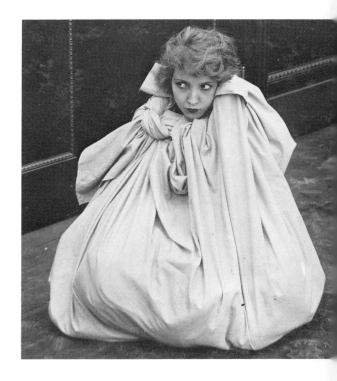

Fairbanks showing his skill with spinning the rope. The strange objects on the right are the inflatable rubber fish used in The Mystery Of The Leaping Fish

The McCarthy brothers, in charge of our Effects Department, invented six-foot-long inflated rubber flying fish with outspread fins on which you could lie and ride the waves or sit and paddle about. I hope they patented the idea: now you can get any kind of inflatable animal to swim on, but they thought of it first.

One scene we shot in Chinatown, using the exterior of a small Chinese laundry. Headed by Bill Lowery, the 'villains', having kidnapped me in a sheet to make me look like a bundle of dirty linen, were to take me inside to have me polished off, not tidied up. Maybe we'd neglected to ask permission to take the scene there or something. Anyway, as Bill carried me through the entrance, war broke out and a great many people went for him. Bill's big boxing mitts were immobilized by me, wriggling and kicking to free myself. I should be grateful he didn't drop me. Tied securely in my sheet, I was unable to see out, and though there was nothing wrong with my hearing I had no idea what was going on – I didn't speak Chinese, unlike everyone else in the room. Not until I was safely deposited on the sidewalk outside and the boys were discussing what had happened did I find out. Chinatown was still anti-American at that time. We were always showing the Chinese as villains in pictures – there was never an oriental hero until Sessue Hayakawa came along and bowled us over – and for us to make use of their shop without even getting permission was the last chop-stick.

Often I went to open the Fairbanks films I was in. These events were always arranged by and for the studio Publicity Department. My singing instructor Mr Constantino must have believed in putting to work as much as we'd accomplished, for at Clune's Broadway, for the opening of *The Good Bad Man*, I sang 'The Rosary' (after the film), complete with gestures – kissing the crucifix, that sort of thing. My family cried, of course, and our friend Marion Strauch from Publicity cried also. The audience was kind, and I was given flowers. Someone had told me to give a rose to the conductor – I thought it a silly idea, but reached down to the pit and did as I'd been told. The audience stood and applauded to a man. They liked my gesture more than my singing. Afterwards Marion said, still misty-eyed, it was so like me. I didn't have the heart to tell her the truth.

Mr Fairbanks had the idea of making films abroad, still with me as his lead (his wife and family would go along too). He loved to go places and wanted to make a complete story in every country he visited. Such an idea was unheard of then, except strictly for travelogues. He must have changed his mind – I only made three films with him. The day after we finished the last one, I went into *Stranded* with De Wolf Hopper, directed by Lloyd Ingraham. I played a trapeze artist on a cheap Variety bill, who falls, is hurt, and has to stay put in a small town.

With De Wolf Hopper, Tom Wilson and Frank Bennett in Stranded

Above: *B.L. in bearskin, startling her chaperone in* Hell-To-Pay-Austin. Left: *The tear-jerking scene in* Hell-To-Pay-Austin

Tall Mr Hopper had no hair on the top of his head – or indeed, anywhere else on his head. I used to think he *must* be wearing a wig; when I think of it now, it was quite obvious. He had an expression which Mr Ingraham used to call 'peeling his eyeballs' to express surprise or shock, like Frankie Howerd with his sudden scared-horse expression. In the middle of a take Mr Ingraham would say to him, 'Now peel the eyeballs!' Mr Hopper would, and it was *very* funny.

Two weeks after *Stranded* was finished I was cast in *Hell-To-Pay-Austin*, opposite Wilfred Lucas, directed by Paul Powell, and we went on location to the northern part of the state. Getting to play the waif in this was a story in itself, even taking well into account that it was my mother who told it and who may have exaggerated just a little bit (say a hundred per cent). The scene was a real tear-jerker: a dirty-faced little mountain waif (me) in rags, wearing men's shoes, bare arms in the sun, long unkempt hair flying in the wind, gathering wild flowers, comes down towards the camera which shows in the foreground her objective – a new-made grave. She arranges the flowers and prays, not silently but importunately, face upturned not only for better light for the camera but in her endeavour to speak to her dead mother 'up there somewhere'.

There were no lines; it was all done *ad lib*. I just pleaded with her, told her in pretty graphic detail how it was now, without her, and tried to persuade her to come back. Everyone around the camera was crying – Mr Powell, my mother (of course), the assistants, the crew – and me? Niagara was a piker – this was *big* water!

When the scene was over and the number being taken, Mr Powell plucked my mother's arm and walked with her a few paces away, saying he had a confession to make. He explained that since I was the 'new girl' on the lot he had not thought I would be able to handle my part and had tried earnestly to have me replaced. Unable to do so, he thought the only way to prove to the studio that he was right and they were wrong was to take the most difficult scene first – this one at the grave – and let the studio see for itself. Bless his heart! He saw for himself, and admitted it.

Chapter Six

FROM APPLYING FOR A JOB AND making a test or, as Mother said, 'being put to the test', then wondering if I was ever actually going to work or merely grow old on the payroll, once I got on that merry-go-round it really did whirl. By the end of my first year I was a veteran of no less than ten films, excluding the scenes I did in *Intolerance*. At this point I was given my first feature role. And isn't it frightening how little remarks give away our real nature and attitudes? At the time I underlined 'featured' in my photograph album, implying that I should have been starred.

A Sister Of Six was one of the first full-length features made by Sidney Franklin and his brother Chester. The Franklin brothers had been making one- and two-reelers for Mr Griffith with the Fine Arts kiddies, who ranged from three to about eight years old. They all had mothers or chaperones in attendance. Six of these youngsters were in our film and I was the Sister of Six. Ralph Lewis played my uncle, his brother Ben played my father and Frank Bennett was the leading man.

It was a romance of rich, early California – hoop skirts, ruffled pantalettes and pretty nightcaps. I played a wealthy young lady from back East who, on the death of my father, comes West to live with the wicked uncle, bringing six little brothers and sisters. (I was always coming West from the East, or vice versa.) This teenage sister is a demure little lady who has to shoot – and kill – the villain, a blond Spaniard with sideburns and a flat, baubled hat played by Al Sears. With a shotgun to back her up, the little lady keeps pleading with him not to come nearer. When he persists, she pulls the trigger and for some reason is surprised and upset to see the untidy result. Such were films out home in our century's teenage.

The pretty *hacienda* set, in the beautiful rolling hill country of the Lasky ranch, was built in typical Colonial Spanish style with a high-walled courtyard and fountain (fake) and an enormous parrot (real), balconies

B.L. playing A Sister of Six *with a gaggle of Fine Arts kiddies. Violet Radcliffe (on B.L.'s left, looking straight to camera) was always cast as a boy.*

and outside stairways. There was one little lady, playing somebody's aristocratic mother – she was an 'older' woman but not as old as she was made up to appear (if you played someone's mother then, you had white hair, stooped and walked with a stick). She had travelled all over the world, while I had never been out of the Southwest, and she never tired of my questions. On those hot, dry, dusty days, we talked for hours when we were not needed in the scenes, sitting in the shade of the (fake) high walls, fanned by the light breeze. And I in turn used to tell endless stories to the six children while they were waiting around.

A lot of time was wasted in those days by working away from the studio in natural settings. You could never judge the time needed, especially with a good company who could afford perfection. It might cloud over or rain in the middle of a scene. Now, with strong lights and the present film stock, you can shoot through it unless it's a monsoon. Then, you were obliged to wait, perhaps for days, for it to clear, returning to the studio at night and coming back every following day until you got what you came for.

You can't start a scene with the sun in the east and finish with the sun in the west, unless it is supposed to take all day. The source of light has to match. And everyone has to be called, in case the weather breaks and their scenes can be taken. And there were no camera scripts then. I remember Sidney and Chet figuring out certain shots they wanted to take that day and writing them down in the car on the way to location. That gives some idea of how swiftly film technique was developing. The close-up itself was still in swaddling clothes. But our young rebels – creative writers, cutters, directors – had the clear vision that too much attention was being paid to continuity for its own sake. Except for Mr Griffith – he couldn't have cared less. He made close-ups of his heroines against something plain and dark, and used back-lighting, regardless of the weather. But, my goodness! What he showed you was worth watching.

In looking up my old photograph album, I see beside the first still from *A Sister Of Six*: 'Began rehearsals, August 4, 1916'; also that the cameraman was 'Mr Able'. I'm glad I was so respectful but Mr Ab*el* would have laughed at my spelling. Like many others in the early film business he was a foreigner, with a thick accent. To let Sidney know the scene was full in, or not, he would say, 'Fadhink hin', or 'Fadhink hout'.

Since films were silent, stage directions were given audibly, sometimes almost in your ear if it was a very close close-up. While you were playing the scene for all it was worth – with real tears – you would hear the director: 'He is gone. He will never come back. You love him so much. You cannot bear it. You pray that he will come back. Pray a little more to the right – no, no – your left . . . You know your prayer is answered. He *will* come back. You are happy – but still crying – now for joy . . . ' 'Fadhink hout.'

'Fadhink hin' became a by-word in the company, and at home we never said anything else when something was about to happen or someone was approaching. The last helping of apple pie would be announced by: 'Fadhink hout!'

Long before I entered films, Mother wrote scenarios and sent them to different studios, which always rejected them. Whether or not the stories were used is another matter. At that time many studios advertised for scripts, rejected them, then without payment or acknowledgement made them into films. Some of those film studios were a shoddy lot; they had very little money to squander on such luxuries as stories. Few of their wares have survived, but if you do see cheap films from those days you may well be seeing a hair-raising, unpaid-for melodrama by my mother.

When I went to work at Griffith's she sent stories to the Script Department. The answer was always, 'No: too melodramatic'. We didn't know what that meant, not that it mattered; we would have just said it was all blood-and-thunder. I'm sure Mother's stories *were* melodramatic; nonetheless, two of them were made into films by my beloved Griffith studio. I once heard Mr Woods, head of the Scenario Department, explain to Mother that very often an idea hits the world in several places at the same time – he was probably telling Mother that her story was not

B.L. playing the name part in Nina The Flower Girl, *exhibited on a stage at a dinner party. The story was Mother's, but the idea of the gold frame was mine*

the one they used for Mae Marsh. But frankly, it seems more than a coincidence considering that they even used Mother's title, *The Wild Girl*, but added *Of The Sierras*.

I played the name part in the other one they used, *Nina The Flower Girl*, for which I started rehearsing in November 1916. I doubt if Mother was paid or even given screen credit because she was not officially a scenario writer.

Nina is a blind flower seller, engaged for one evening as entertainment for an expensive party. She is one of the items exhibited on a little stage, appearing with her basket of flowers in a large gold frame, to look like a framed picture. The story was Mother's but the idea of the framed picture was mine. The story goes that a very drunk gentleman takes a fancy to Nina. He thinks the blindness is feigned, and chases Nina through the house and out of a French window, which happens to be open and unbalconied. (The ending, surprisingly enough, is a happy one.)

Lloyd Ingraham was the director. He'd had years of experience as a stage actor, and in early Biograph films as an actor and director. He had an eccentric way of working; he cussed a fair amount and had an imaginative longshoreman's vocabulary in describing a scene. But he always treated me as a child, telling me about Mary Pickford, whom he had worked with at Biograph, and imitating her voice and her way of holding

68

her head on one side as she spoke. Once when a young man on the set asked me back to his flat for a drink, Mr Ingraham screwed up his face and said, 'No! No! No! No! *No*! She's just a kid!' To which the young man quickly added, 'Well, she could have a glass of milk.'

When we reached the scene of the big gold frame, Mr Ingraham told me very sweetly what they had in mind – me with the flower basket, framed like a picture on the stage, and so on. Yes, I said, I knew. It was my idea. This set him back only a little, because I think he thought I didn't understand him. He began again to tell me and I interrupted him again to say I *knew* all that; it was my idea in the first place . . . Fortunately for the safety of the studio, Elmer Clifton's wife Adele, who played a small part in the film, tactfully led me away until the set could cool down and production be resumed.

Mr Ingraham had little respect for anyone except Mr Griffith. Whenever the top brass came on the set to see how it was humming, he would stop work, say in a loud voice, 'Watch out! We must look busy!', and start running round in circles, adjusting things, rushing back and forth to the camera, peering from every angle, generally cluttering up everything and not turning a crank until the visitors retreated, laughing.

We didn't have written lines as for a play at the Griffith studio, but used natural dialogue – which, after all, doesn't alter much: 'Close the window, please' is the same as saying, 'Would you mind shutting the window' – unless a word cue had to be given for, say, the firing of a gun or an actor's entrance.

The Griffith studio had a pretty serious approach to work. There were exceptions – if the actors were bored, they might make some remark like, 'Well, enjoy yourself!' while adjusting the noose on the poor wretch standing over the trap door. But a well-established company interested in making money did not find such remarks funny. Don't forget the lip-readers in the audience – if, during a passionate love scene, the leading man was flip enough to criticize the fastening on the back of the leading lady's dress: 'Your pins are sticking in my hand!' it would have been quickly reported to the studio by irate devotees of film 'art'.

Wild Irish Eddie Dillon, an excitable young director who had been an even younger actor at the Biograph, directed me in *The Heiress At Coffee Dan's* and *A Daughter Of The Poor*. While directing any scene Eddie, behind the camera, always acted every part. During a fight he nearly knocked himself out. I thought some bits highly tragic, and played them thus, but both films were hilarious comedies. While we were making *A Daughter Of The Poor* with Roy Stewart, George Beranger and Max Davidson, a favourite comic, other actors on the lot used to come and watch for the outrageous things I would say. I never used bad language: to me a villain was, 'You dirty dog!' . . . 'How dare you!' I would add, for good measure. Our impromptu audience spared me nothing and howled with laughter. They never knew what was coming out next any more than I did.

With Georgie Stone in A Daughter Of The Poor, *directed by Eddie Dillon*

As long as it looked realistic, dialogue didn't matter so much in thrillers. Instead of real lines some actors concentrated on the action, merely saying – literally – 'So and so and so-and-so and so! So?' Ford Sterling and many other comics worked this way in slapstick. Who cared? You were far too busy watching what they were doing and laughing too hard to notice. Lillian Gish and Bobby Harron did the same in their young-love scenes, both of them whispering charming, dreamy sweet nothings at the same time, neither listening to the other.

Most directors in those days went through scenes beforehand to show you what they meant – acting it all out, even when they were atrocious actors. Now that's considered bad form – ham, amateur – but I still like it. Mr Griffith always worked that way. While he was going through it to show you, he was almost incoherent, but he felt and conveyed to you what he meant as no other director I have worked with has ever done. Sometimes, watching rehearsals, he would cover his ears to make sure the meaning of the scene was clear without words or sound. It's a good idea – Joseph Henabery, who began with Griffith, did the same when I worked with him later in New York.

To help actors get into the mood of a scene, we had atmospheric music, a two- or three-piece orchestra, on the sidelines of the set. Sometimes they carried on between scenes to keep everybody from going stale; sometimes they played while the scene was being shot; and it was heaven at the end of a day when your spirits were flagging.

At the Fine Arts studio we had a small orchestra. Rhea Haines, a pretty brunette, was a pianist and talented musician as well as an actress. Violinist Jimmy Mason was also an actor. Through Rhea we all met Speed Hansen from Lasky's studio. Speed, so called because of a song, 'Ella Speed', which we made him sing incessantly, was a guitarist; easygoing, good-natured, fun to have around.

Commodore J. Stuart Blackton, a big shot from Vitagraph (I worked with him later on *The American*, a forerunner of 3-D and The Big Screen), always had the same singer to provide the music on his sets at Vitagraph. She accompanied herself on the melodian with one hand while holding a small megaphone in the other, crooning in unobtrusive contralto. Most effective.

At that time the fad was to take your ukelele with you wherever you went and play for everybody to sing. You've no idea how popular you were if you had any kind of repertoire. We swopped songs and chords, all by ear. I learned to play on a terapache, eight-stringed instead of four, and slightly larger than a uke. My terapache cost four dollars – you could have found something for less but I've never heard anything like its mellow tone. It's mahogany and was once a chopping block at the back door of a boy's house. He made it himself and I think he must have carved one side at a time – though each is in perfect proportion, one side is Mae West, the other Baby Peggy.

A jam session between scenes on Purple Dawn

Chapter Seven

WHEN, IN 1917, D. W. GRIFFITH
left Triangle Corporation, I was automatically released from my personal
contract with him. John Quinn, who worked for the company, left it to
become my personal manager and promptly signed me back on the
pay-roll, this time at Ince's (another point of the Triangle, by then in
Culver City) at five times the salary I had been paid at Fine Arts. Paul
Powell came to direct me in *The Sawdust Ring*, and I told him how sad I was
that Mr Griffith had not asked me to join his new company. 'Oh yes he
did,' was his reply. 'No,' I repeated, 'I was never asked.' 'Oh yes, you
were,' he insisted, his whole face crinkling up as he delightedly puffed at
his cigarette. Mr Griffith must have got him to quiz me and in this way
discovered that I was already signed up.

Mr Quinn had firm views on how things should be done. He was a tight
disciplinarian, with himself as well as with everybody else, and one of the
first things he instructed me to do was never to make friends with anyone
working with or for me. In this way it never became difficult to criticize or
even fire them. But it also meant that I was never to accept social
invitations from members of the company, not even from the director.

Another thing *verboten* by Mr Quinn was riding horseback, skiing or any
potentially dangerous sports. Suppose something happened to you in the
middle of a film? My first winter in New York, working for Pathé, I was
dying to try ice-skating. Mr Quinn found out and said, 'What happens if
you fall down and everybody skates over your face?' So I didn't go
ice-skating. This can be inhibiting because then you're not just a dumb
blonde; you become a stupid dumb blonde, and an unhappy one at that.

It was probably Mr Quinn's lack of theatrical experience which caused
him to make some mistakes. But it is too easy to blame someone else for
things going wrong. We had an office in New York – I don't think I paid
for it; he did. He paid for expensive full back-page advertisements in the

important trade publications like *Motion Picture Magazine* – something normally done only by large studios, not by individuals – to give me status. He negotiated all my contracts, of course; he advised me to break my contract with Ince and go to New York with Pathé, which I did. Then there was a contract with Vitagraph on the West Coast. Here is where his talents shone: I had the right to choose my leading man, stories, the lot.

We bought books to make into films; I'm sure I didn't pay for any of these. We took options on books like *The Enchanted Barn*, which I recommended to Vitagraph. But I don't think he had a good idea of what would make a successful film. On some of my pictures for Vitagraph a separate sub-title all by itself read, 'Supervised by Bessie Love' (or some such phrase). When I first saw it I thought, 'Where did that come from?' Mr Quinn was non-committal. Maybe it was the studio's way of saying they were not responsible for it. It might not have been such a compliment as it seems.

How much salary you receive doesn't matter. How much you have left after even legitimate expenses is frightening. Very early in my working life I was launched with a personal manager, a personal publicity agent and one of the best cameramen in the business, Clyde de Vinna. Vitagraph were not used to spending money on production and refused to pay Clyde's salary. He had left Ince to come to me, so I made up the difference.

Whenever working in New York, I lived with Mother at the Biltmore Hotel – a little like the Ritz, only bigger. Out home we always rented tasteful furnished houses, had the necessary servants to run them, and owned a car (beside Dad's Hupmobile). Then we – that is, I – began buying a house in Hollywood and a dairy in Pixley, above Bakersfield, 150 miles from Los Angeles.

In about 1918, my manager and I agreed to end our association. The best contract in the world is not the whole answer: you must also have someone with good judgement, wisdom and experience, who knows how to use it. This was just three years since I'd been in high school. You don't really become a theatrical – or a financial – wizard in three years. Besides paying him the usual ten per cent due weekly on my salary I now agreed to pay off, also weekly, the ten per cent which would be due in the future, beginning at the end of the Vitagraph contract, working backwards to the present time until it met up with itself. In other words, twenty per cent every week.

Then a company was formed to make films with me: Callaghan Productions. Within a year or so, with my running expenses increasing weekly, the Callaghan contract ended and I found myself unemployed for the first time. This was catastrophic. There were so many obligations, like Molochs demanding their sacrifices: no assembly-line could have kept up with them. The telephone was cut off at my home in Laurel Canyon, and so was the water supply. Then word reached me late one evening that Dad was critically ill at the dairy in Pixley and should be brought home.

Arriving in New York with, on B.L.'s left, Mr John Quinn

I still had my personal maid, whose husband was the chauffeur. Goodness knows when they had last been paid. But the chauffeur wasn't there; anyway I doubt if there was petrol in the car, which was a big Winton town car, chauffeur-driven only. Yet somehow I had to get to Pixley and bring my father home.

Irving Thalberg had called to see me that evening and was there when word came about my father. Irving was a beau of mine: not serious, but a beau. He was a sweet boy with good manners, who blushed easily. So did I. He was then in his late teens and in charge of Universal City, the sprawling studio in the San Fernando valley, just over the hills. Whenever you hear of Irving Thalberg being a boy genius, running a studio, settling labour disputes *and* making good films, you are hearing the truth.

Irving was new to Hollywood. He knew nothing of California distances and drove quite a modest car. Even so, when you divide his chivalry in half and take away another quarter for his ignorance, he was still gallant. He immediately said we would go that minute and fetch Dad. On my word, I really did try to dissuade him. I didn't know what on earth I was going to do, but I was not insensible of the sacrifice it would entail for him. I was not certain that he knew just how much he was offering. He was adamant. We would go right then! So we did.

After about a hundred miles or so he began asking how much further it was. By then it was too late to turn back, though we still had quite a way to go. At last we passed through Bakersfield. Dawn began to break and suddenly he realized what day it now was at the studio – pay day, and he had to sign the salary cheques!

Just before we reached Pixley – our ranch was a little way outside the town – he made me promise one thing. Gently, but quite firmly, he said that no matter what news awaited us, he must make a telephone call to the studio cashier. I most meekly agreed. We arrived at the Pixley Post Office, and were given the full news about my father – sunstroke: he was unconscious. I started for the door when Irving quietly reminded me: 'The telephone?' 'Oh, yes.' – He phoned, made his arrangements and we went on to the ranch. A young farmer neighbour made a bed in his big car and brought Dad down to Hollywood after we returned home later that day. Dad stayed until he was better, nursed by Clara, my maid, and then went back to work on the ranch.

The bottom drops out of the career of an actor – and you can usually time it – about every five years. Not just periodic unemployment, but the end of everything. In 1920 – five years after my film début – I had my first taste of this.

At this bleakest of moments, Sessue Hayakawa – America's first 'Chinese' screen hero, though in fact he was Japanese – asked me to play opposite him in *The Swamp*. This was a new role for me – an unmarried mother. Without any designs on my part, I was entering my new Five Year Plan.

After playing an *ingénue* in *The Sea Lion*, cast as the daughter of Hobart Bosworth, the captain of a whaler, and still paying on a house for us and a barn for the cows, I took anything to keep going. There were a couple of two-reelers (I'd never made a two-reel film before) in a series of westerns with Tom Santschi and Ruth Stonehouse, followed by a small part in *Three Who Paid* which was so small I can't remember what it was.

Forget-Me-Not came in there somewhere, produced by Louis Burston and directed by Woody Van Dyke, and it was a honey. Gareth Hughes and I played children in an orphanage. Woody and the camera department invented a very moving effect for the scene when I had to cry as Gareth is adopted by my mother, who does not know me and refuses to adopt me because I am crippled. Woody cut from me crying to Gareth leaving, and to give the impression of my tearful view of his departure, dripped castor oil down a slide in front of the camera lens. A great success.

In 1921 I was in *The Vermilion Pencil*, playing opposite Sessue Hayakawa again. The story was of Old China turning into New China: a mandarin buying a rough mountain girl (me) and attempting to make her a silken

Off set with director Rowland V. Lee during filming of The Sea Lion, *made on board a whaling ship*

lady. Then I meet Sessue, the New China student of engineering, out in the mountains, building viaducts, bridges and tunnels.

The Vermilion Pencil was made in pre-bob days and we knew of no temporary hair dye, so for the unkempt mountain girl I painted my long thick hair with mascara. What mascara does for eyelashes – makes them black and stiff – it did to my hair. It was also like indelible lipstick which rubs off everywhere but won't come off when you want it to. I had to sleep with my head in a towel.

Then came my transformation into the silken witch in brocade trouser suits. The studio found a Chinese hairdresser for me – dear Mrs Wong Wing. Undaunted by that mat I had concocted, she persevered until she could pull the comb straight through my hair without taking my head back with it. Next she slapped on bandolin which she made then and there out of bamboo shavings and water (at that time we used tiny dabs of prepared bandolin to keep chic spit-curls – kiss-curls – in place). Putting it on with a trowel like this meant that everything was plastered into place and set like cement. Before my unbelieving gaze, too late to do anything but gasp, I watched the lady paint my hair jet black. I didn't know what she was using – but by then it didn't matter. I could see my fair self as permanently black.

However, Mrs Wong assured me in broken English that I would not explode, shrink or disintegrate as a result, so I let her get on with it. It went on and on – it was probably torture, I don't remember, but I shall never forget the effect. As well as all sorts of elaborate dressings and twistings to the top-knot, birds, beads, ivory combs and jade hairpins were added . . . it was endless and out of this world.

Our location had by now moved to an exquisite Japanese house on top of a hill, smack in the middle of Hollywood. It belonged to two German brothers called Bernheimer, gifted linguists and importers of oriental goods. In my make-up, complete with baubles and brocades, I was introduced there to one of the brothers and a friend. As we were talking, my host suddenly asked where I was born. When I said Texas, he said, 'Oh? Then had I learned English in this country?' His friend had to remind him that though Love was a common name among the Chinese, this was Miss *Bessie* Love and they had *often* seen *her* on the screen. I was still pondering this at the end of the day when I opened the door at home and my mother didn't recognize me at all . . . I guess it was a good make-up.

In 1922 I was another Chinese in *Purple Dawn* – of all titles – directed by the unstoppable Charlie Seeling, cameraman on some of my Vitagraph pictures. Bill Aldrich, a friend of mine, played the sailor I was hopelessly in love with. In the plot I save his life, hand him over to his blonde fiancée, and walk into San Francisco Bay.

Apart from very special make-up effects like my Chinese transformation by Mrs Wong, when I went to work all actors used to make themselves up and dress their own hair. They used the cheapest brand make-

Purple Dawn, *saving the life of the sailor played by Bill Aldrich*

up – Stein's greasepaint sticks, powder in tins and lip-rouge in little jars furrowed down the sides to look like cut glass. The greasepaint was a shade of yellow and had a strange, penetrating smell. By 1917 we were going to ordinary hairdressers outside the studio before coming to work and by the Twenties we had our own – the best – full-time on the lot.

We all used to plaster on our lip-rouge for glamour, but no good cameraman would allow it. They made us take it off – the slightest tinge of red, even orange, photographed jet black. The Owl Drug Store removal cream was used with rags to get it off. Lipstick was as yet unknown. (The mother of director Preston Sturges invented indelible lipstick. She was one of the Isadora Duncan dancers in Paris.)

I saw Barbara LaMarr freshening her face at a party one night. She was one of the world's most beautiful women, from the top of her expensively waved dark hair to her extravagant pedicure. She was carrying a 14-carat gold-mesh handbag with a tiny rouge compartment in the clasp. I watched in the mirror as she carefully smeared her natural rose-bud mouth a gorgeous crimson. 'Barbara,' I said, 'do tell me what make rouge that is.' She left the 'pinkie painter' mid-air and turned that generous, all-embracing smile full on me: 'Jus' Stein's, honey.'

Hot-black cosmetic – black greasepaint – was melted over a candle, then applied with an eyelash brush, instead of mascara. You were careful not to touch the lashes once they were done, as the black would smear easily.

Smearing make-up reminds me: it became a routine in one company I was in. Come the end of the day, one of my attackers would say to the director, 'Finished?' If he waited for a reply, he was already too late – I was fleeing the set. If they caught me, they would smear the black make-up down my whole face. I was never hurt, but I certainly looked like something the cat brought in.

A fair amount of make-up – not mine – was smeared one time in a production. It was not unknown during filming for your friends to 'frame' someone by saying there was a new scene added and then, without any film in the camera, get them to enact the most hair-raising nonsense or the most outrageous love scene. This last was what happened in *Carolyn Of The Corners*. I was Carolyn, a child newly orphaned. Charles Edler (my Uncle Joe in the film), with the help of director Bob Thornby and cameraman Frank B. Good, had framed tall, beautiful, auburn-haired Charlotte Mineau, who played the part of my kind grown-up friend secretly in love with Uncle Joe. I suppose she thought it only natural that they should have a love scene for a happy ending. There followed as torrid a one as no censor would have passed, Charlotte's make-up spreading all over both their faces. I'm sure she too thought it was funny – afterwards.

There must be something about make-up which brings out the practical joker in people. Bill Wellman was assistant director to Colin Campbell for *Three Who Paid*, made in about 1922 for Fox. I was disguised as a boy, and had forgotten to bring spirit gum to hold down the hairline of my boy's wig. Bill suggested the prop man would probably have LePage's glue in his box.

'Oh, Bill! That holds furniture together.' That's all Bill needed. 'Oh, they use it for wigs, too.' 'You're kidding!' 'No, no. Try it and see.' I had to do something, so I asked the prop man. He must have thought I was out of my head. Anyway, LePage's (furniture) glue was applied. I worked all day, came home, and tried to take off my wig. It was at that moment that I realized what a good laugh they all must have had. And do you wonder that I always looked a little sideways at *anyone* offering to help me in *any* situation?

Cecil B. De Mille once said to me after one of those looks of mine, 'Were you weaned on a lemon?' He said it with a twinkle, but he said it.

All the first parts I played were character *ingénues* – much more fun than vacuous straight leads – and right from the beginning I had a flair for finding character wardrobe. I bought a pair of sticking-out shoes, with the soles flapping, straight off the feet of a small boy in Fountain Avenue. When this small boy grew up to be a tall electrician, working in the studios, he reminded me of it.

I used some of my own wardrobe in *Acquitted*, my third film. The studio

Painting our home at Laurel Canyon

had plenty of money but they went in more for realism, and my own clothes were typical of the daughter of a lower-middle-class white-collar worker. I wore a white starched Dutch-shaped bonnet, turned up at the corners, which I had made, embroidered, washed and cold-starched myself. And though parasols went out with Queen Victoria, in the film I carried my own painted silk one. The butterflies and forget-me-nots don't show in the stills because pale colours didn't photograph, but they're there.

Again, I used my own clothes for a scene in the Modern period of *Intolerance* – a black-and-white checked skirt and jacket which Mother had had altered to fit me. The scene was nothing – just me listening outside the telephone booth of a station waiting-room. I am supposed to be sitting asleep, my baby brother sleeping beside me. A man runs wildly to the telephone, gets the Governor of the State on the line, demands a stay of execution for Bobby Harron – he is not guilty! To convey what is happening, the film being silent, Mr Griffith shows the effect on someone outside (me in the waiting-room), waking up wide-eyed at what she hears.

At the Griffith studio, the Stock Wardrobe for Crowd Artistes and character parts was transformed after a streetcar mishap threatened to end the career of a German actor named Curt Rehfeld. When he returned to the studio after losing a leg in the accident, he was put in charge of the wardrobe. There was nothing helpless about his approach to his new job! He had the whole place scrubbed from ceiling to floor; divisions, shelves, cubicles and cupboards made for different categories of costume. Everything was inventoried; all character clothes were sent to the wet-wash laundry and left unironed so they looked crumpled and dirty but would not, frankly, smell. (Long afterwards, in Brecht's *St Joan* at the Queen's Theatre, London, when I complained about the smelly sacks tied around us 'poor', I was told rather tartly that they were *supposed* to be dirty. Such indignity is surely unnecessary – any actor can act smelly without ponging clean across the pit.)

In the Modern Wardrobe at Griffith's we had costumes worn by the great stage actress Madame Modjeska, who had bought a ranch in California when she retired from the theatre. These were beautiful costumes from her performances in classical plays, and were handled with loving care by the ladies in the wardrobe, as were the famous ones from Madame Clara Butt, who'd always used more than one per recital.

You have ambition and wish to put running legs under it? If you have the spirit of romance, courage, daring, determination – you're halfway there. In 1922 Douglas Fairbanks, Sr, had just made *Robin Hood* and had gone off to enjoy the fruits of it. The parents of a little boy named Arthur Trimble wanted to put him in films – enough to pay to do it. And Fred Becker, an actor from *Robin Hood*, hankered after being a director. There you have the first two ingredients of a film production. And finally, there were all those gorgeous medieval accoutrements specially made for the Fairbanks epic, which would now be available to all comers.

With Arthur Trimble, using cast and costumes from Douglas Fairbanks' Robin Hood *in*
The Adventures Of Prince Courageous

The entire cast except the boy and me were small-part players from
Robin Hood so they all went back to wearing the same costumes they'd
been pulling up and over for weeks. And what imagination with the sets! A
Robin Hood window frame and sweeping velvet curtain made our 'corner of
the castle'; with Robin's 'stone walls', some props and a couple of horses,
you had a courtyard; the shadow of some iron bars made a prison. I don't
remember a big set of any kind. It all went to save money and produce a
series of child adventures which every small boy fancies himself undertak-
ing. These fairy stories, *The Adventures Of Prince Courageous*, were not
important in film history, but they were among the happiest engagements
I've ever had.

Relaxing after shooting Slave of Desire. *From left: Director George Baker, Carmel Myers, Eulalie Jensen, B.L.*

Chapter Eight

HAVING BEGUN AT THE TOP, BY the early Twenties I was working my way down, taking anything to keep the wolves from whelping on my doorstep. I did *Bulldog Courage*, a western quickie, all white riding breeches and desperadoes, with George Larkin. Then I had a dramatic role in *The Village Blacksmith* ('Under The Spreading Chestnut Tree . . . ' by Mr Longfellow) at Fox, where John Ford wouldn't allow me to bring my uke on to the set. This was too hard. With experience you learn to take knocks as they come, but after being out of work too long you lose your cool. I was already hypersensitive about some of the bad films I'd made – and I'm afraid some were stinkeroo – and it didn't help to have salt sprinkled over and then rubbed in in case the scars didn't show.

People often ask me, 'Wasn't life easier in silent films?' When I was making *St Elmo* at Fox in 1923, the electricians were trying to form a union. On this picture we worked all one day, and through the night until two or three the next morning. I was allowed to go home to get some rest as I was the leading lady. But Jack Gilbert, playing St Elmo, was supposed to look haggard. So he went on shooting, with only a couple of hours' break. After they'd finished both that day and that night, the electricians went from the studio to the location, set up the lights and reflectors, and by then it was time for the rest of us to begin again. The crew were still at it from the day before. When they went to collect their overtime, the studio said, 'Oh, no. Overtime finished last night at twelve o'clock. This is now the next day. You're just working a regular shift.'

After *St Elmo*, up jumped the devil. If your unemployment coincided with a visit from the Wall Street efficiency experts to teach us how to make motion pictures, it was murder. The studios would close down, for a start. This must have been one of their visitations, because all the major

Above: *with John Gilbert in* St Elmo. Below: *as a drug addict in* Human Wreckage

companies were closed, and everybody was on this unemployed boat – directors, writers, cameramen, the lot.

If you want to stay in the business, you can try adopting a new character for yourself, and keep trying until you establish yourself in it. Cut out all luxuries, bar none. Cut down on food if you must but never appear to be hard-up. Just follow the same routine as anyone else who is down on his uppers.

Eventually I did a quickie, *Deserted At The Altar*, for Phil Goldstone. Proper salaries were paid but we shot it in ten days: no re-takes, no close-ups, no rehearsals. You can only do that with pros. Our director, William K. Howard (*Fire Over England*), and the cast were all well known, established players including Frankie Lee, the child actor.

In *Ghost Patrol* at Universal I played opposite Ralph Graves. Nick Grinde was the assistant director; when I had bouts of illness during the shooting, he carried me through the rain from my dressing-room to the set. Such action shots get you to know people quickly . . .

Things had been picking up, but not enough to wait around for them. I now did a few cameos – tiny parts, dramatic scene-stealers. This happens all the time to older players who can't get a job any other way, not usually to well-known youngsters. But by now I was an old hand, even though I was still a young one. When the studios saw I was willing, one cameo led to another until life was one Victorian necklace.

Fallen women and wives seemed to come next. Marshall 'Mickey' Neilan warned me about the part of the nice secretary whose virtue slipped in *The Eternal Three*; audiences used to associate a role with the actor playing it, and Mickey was afraid for my reputation. My part was not the lead, but I was overjoyed to work under his direction. Having survived that fallen peach, I played a drug addict for Tom Ince in *Human Wreckage*, a propaganda film against narcotics. All my best friends warned me I would be accused of being one but none of it seemed to harm me.

After *Slave Of Desire* (*The Magic Skin*), from *The Wild Ass's Skin* by Balzac, at Goldwyn, Rowland V. Lee had me play the title role of *Gentle Julia*, as a middle-west small-town charmer. Although I was still freelancing, I now worked for a year for First National, a conglomerate of independent producers. First, *Torment* with Maurice Tourneur; then *Those Who Dance* (the first version), playing a gangster's moll for Tom Ince. The star was my best friend Blanche Sweet, with Warner Baxter; Lambert Hillyer directed. I couldn't have done better. After that *Dynamite Smith*, again for Ince, with Charlie Ray, Wallace Beery and Jacqueline Logan.

Instead of too little work, I suddenly had too much again. While working in the daytime on *Dynamite Smith* at Ince's Culver City studio, and at night on *A Woman On The Jury* with Lew Cody and Sylvia Breamer at First National in Hollywood, at noon I was fitting clothes and hair and reading the script for *Sundown*, also to be made for First National, on location in Texas. I was to leave immediately my shots in both the other films were finished and checked for re-takes. When did I sleep? Oh, that!

At last my moonlighting for *Sundown* was finished and in March I could leave with the rest of the company for Texas: big, big, flat, empty Texas, with nothing on it except us and a great deal of fine sand which blew about at the slightest zephyr. Even the wagon road used to follow the whims of these *mistrals* from day to day. One day someone pointed out that as far as the eye could see in this unobstructed vastness we were completely surrounded by baby whirlwinds. When you get enough of these together they quickly grow into a grand-daddy tornado. And would you believe it, we had brought a wind machine! The live wind blew it over when we were shooting one night and made the horses stampede among us and the Klieg lights.

Our location was on a plateau seventy-five miles out from El Paso. They hauled our water nine miles, and the wood for the cook-stove, twelve. Before we left Hollywood, we'd had dreams of sitting around the campfire at night, singing and playing the ukelele. Can you see them letting us have wood for a bonfire? Or sitting around in the open at night? In Texas, in March? We not only had March winds; we had snow, too. Because of the scarcity of water, I had a coconut oil rub every night instead of a bath, and my skin got to be like silk. Who wants a silken skin in the middle of a desert in winter?

When we arrived they put us into tents with little oil heaters. I can believe that fuel oil will not freeze under any conditions, because it remained liquid the whole time we were there. The temperature was the same whether the stove was alight or not. This comic-opera heating arrangement was soon transformed when a wooden shack – a row of rooms – was thrown up for the womenfolk. Until the tar paper came to cover it, the snow came through the cracks in drifts. Then, as if by magic, in the middle of each room was placed the best thing the U.S. Army has ever bestowed on man – an army stove.

A wooden frame about four inches high and two feet square was put on the floor and filled with earth; the open bottom of the stove was set on this earth, and the stove filled with fuel. It had a stove-pipe and a chimney, and made the place like an oven. Stones were placed around the sides to warm and when we went to bed they were wrapped in paper and put at our feet. The bed we also had to learn about: given one army cot, we first spread newspapers on it to keep out the draughts, then opened out one army blanket, made the bed, and finally folded the army blanket over the whole thing like an envelope.

Like most companies when they take a large outfit on such a location, we made a tent city – only the womenfolk had the wooden building – with streets, which everybody had fun in naming. Here we had a regular catering crew with a big dining tent where we all ate together and which, incidentally, blew down – hundreds of square yards of it – during one of the tempests, to be followed by a cold lunch.

Roy Stewart was the leading man. Tall, broad-shouldered, he knew more dialects and laughed harder at his own stories than anyone else.

Our location in Texas for Sundown

Arthur Hoyt played my father. Charlie Murray from Keystone Cops, who had turned straight actor, was with us; so was Hobart Bosworth, the big, handsome screen idol of former days. He was still a heart-breaker with his strong sunburned features and carefully rumpled thick white hair. In town he rode a big grey horse called Cameo.

My wardrobe consisted of a little gingham number and slippers. The howling winds soon took care of that: I wore my bibbed overalls underneath the whole time, and cavalry boots when they were not in shot. The minute the camera stopped, I was wrapped in my fleece-lined army jacket and blankets.

Unlike any sensible location company working deep in the heart of Texas, which would get up at five in the morning and start shooting when it gets light, on *Sundown* we worked studio hours, starting about nine o'clock. The sandstorms always came up around ten, and we had to knock off until they stopped, some time in the afternoon. Anyway, at noon no cameraman will work with the sun directly overhead, casting black shadows under everybody's eyes and making the leading lady look a hundred and six, and the leading man like a gorilla.

We'd left home with the idea of being gone eight days. We stayed eight weeks. I wrote to someone that instead of *Sundown* we were calling it *All Day*. Figuring they had a scoop, they sent this as a news item to the press. Some time later I saw a photograph of myself in a magazine with the astonishing information underneath, 'New title – *All Day*.'

To amuse ourselves we had horse races. The real cowboys removed their boots and stripped their horses, riding without saddle or bridle, yelling like Comanches. We made up an orchestra – me with my ukelele, one of the *vaqueros* (Mexican cowboys) with a guitar, Charlie Murray drumming anything within reach of a couple of knives and forks – and sang Mexican songs and pop tunes. And we had a baseball game, in which I knocked a homer. Two of the boys lifted me off the ground by the braces of my overalls and ran with me from base to base. By the time they threw me home, we were the only people playing – everyone else was cheering.

But we made up for our dallying. Someone at 'the top' must have sent a message and we began to work without stopping for anything, even lunch.

We covered more than Texas to make our film. There had been a drought in the southwest for seven years and we had difficulty in finding enough cattle left in any one place to meet our needs. Vegetation had dried up, then the water-holes had evaporated, and many ranches had lost thousands of head. For our story, which was about the last big cattle drive up the Chisholm Trail, you had to have more than a couple of cows. One way and another our company finally managed to get enough stock together so that, looking down from a mountain, we had seven thousand head in one shot.

On one enormous ranch in Arizona, miles from anywhere, we came across a small shack which was used by the cowhands working the cattle out that way. It was stocked with provisions, like all such shacks in that kind of country – an unwritten law, which I saw in action then, is that whoever comes along can go in and use whatever food is there, but you leave the dishes washed and the place tidy.

My mother always went with me on location. On this occasion Charlie Murray, keeping a straight face, told her that I wanted to know if she'd found the doughnut flour. My mother was a very good cook. 'Doughnut flour?' she asked. There was no such thing. Did I want some doughnuts, she wondered. Charlie said he didn't know, that was all I'd said. Why, yes, Mother said, she'd make some doughnuts. Whereupon she went into that shack and did just that – for all of us. It would never have entered her head to make them just for me. Before you could say, 'Pht!' she was catering for the entire company on that location, and after that we had hot doughnuts every day out there in the middle of that great platter of a place.

My part in *Sundown* had been a leading one. In *A Woman On The Jury* with Sylvia Breamer and Lew Cody, I was back in a supporting role, but like many others I'd been playing the part was too important to be cut down or out. I was discovering that success will never desert you if you can find exciting parts, however small: what *is* agony is to have the camera trained on you for five relentless reels when you have absolutely nothing to do but simper.

I had begun this cameo lark working for very little, but with each succeeding job I doubled the fee. In *The Lost World* the money was all right and the filming took eight weeks. The picture, made in 1925, was a masterpiece of its day, in stop-motion photography with miniature animals and sets. It is still in existence and what with the film societies and TV, I don't think the sun has ever set on it. Lewis Stone and Lloyd Hughes were the older and younger lovers; Wallace Beery and Arthur Hoyt the argumentative professors.

A friend of mine, the Arctic explorer Dr Vilhjalmur Stefansson, was visiting Sir Arthur Conan Doyle when a cheque arrived by post from a film company for rights to *The Lost World*. Sir Arthur couldn't see why they should buy the rights for his book, or how they could photograph it, since it contained a sequence about living prehistoric animals. Dr Stefansson suggested I write about how they made it since I played the leading lady – *any* lady on that safari was news to Sir Arthur.

In the section he was concerned about, some carnivorous animals as tall as St Paul's Cathedral spend their Sundays chewing each other up then pick their teeth. Some of it is pretty grim; but there is also a giant mother-rhino-sort-of-animal with an armour-plated pageboy haircut and a businesslike horn on the end of her nose. Suddenly from under her protecting tummy out trots a baby rhino. The tender, nuzzling affection the special effects men managed to get from those rubber animals was most touching. There were tiny bellows inside the bodies to make them 'breathe'. After they had warmed up under the lights for a while it felt most odd to handle them – especially if you hadn't seen someone sneak over and work the bellows.

There was an enclosure with a shallow tank in the studio where real crocodiles, alligators and an extremely foreign-looking wild pig were running around. One day I dropped my pencil through the slats of a walk built over this pond and, like a fool, reached for it. The alligator was way ahead of me. He snapped the pencil in two, leaving me with my hands intact. And I'd just had a still taken of me sitting on the back of that gentleman!

I used to believe that action films should be made on the location named. Even today most of *The Lost World* looks realistic, and has a steamy atmosphere of dripping moss and leaves and danger. It was actually shot by Arthur Edeson on the back lot of the First National studio (now Paramount) in Hollywood – and by the open sewer of Los Angeles, which ran behind M.G.M. in Culver City. Luckily the camera didn't record odours.

In one scene the canoe I was in had to glide along that sewer under an overhanging 'prop' tree with a real python coiled round it. Now pythons, like anyone else, if given enough beefsteak are quite friendly. But they also happen to be water snakes. This one caught a glimpse of our 'river' flowing beneath the tree and could hardly wait to unbraid herself from her lookout post – and the shot of us gliding towards the camera was so lengthy that no prop man could remain on the scene long enough to keep her in place.

I didn't want to frighten my 'native' scouts, but I'd seen that python unpacked from a large gunny sack. There was a great deal of her and it was all on the tree under which we were to make our way. Our 'natives' were Mexicans from around the Plaza down town and the idea of a real snake being used in a film sent them all into melodious *mestizo* laughter. It stopped when they saw it was true. We gently paddled under and past the swinging live rope, ever swaying nearer our heads. I don't like the idea of being kissed by a python and I think the only thing that kept Juanito from diving overboard was the fact that he couldn't swim. That, and the thought – not a pretty one – of what he would be diving into. And in such company!

At first I was dressed for the part in the usual Hollywood conception of the secretary/heroine, whether she was roughing it in London's West End or in the jungles of South America. I remember a pretty silk blouse trimmed in pleated ruffles. This was before permanent pleats; I don't know how we thought a secretary would keep those pleats in, in a rain forest. And for my hair I had a three-quarter wig as glam as Percy Westmore, the studio hairdresser, could make it. Marion Fairfax ('Dear Miss Fairfax', former confidential columnist) was the producer. She took one look at my silk pleated get-up and said, 'But you look like you're made up for the Follies, dear.' When we asked our technical adviser what he had worn in the jungle he said, 'Pyjamas.' We settled for something plain and a couple of braids.

Did you ever work with a monkey? Don't. This tiny animal produced disastrous effects by ruining the clothes of whoever was holding him. He was palmed off from one to the other of us until he had been through the entire cast. When it came to my turn we had to re-take the scene. The director, Harry Hoyt, said to me, 'You mustn't show that you hate the animal.' 'I love the little thing,' I cried. 'I'm sorry to see it so unhappy with me.'

They showed me the scene. The re-take was for me, not the monkey. He'd bitten me on the finger, but somehow that hadn't come over on film. What *had* come over very sharply was me, all braids and soft focus, threatening to bite him back. Jocko was soon written out of the film and returned to his Hollywood hutch.

Harry Hoyt was an awfully nice man. Self-educated, he once told us a little about his pre-college days. To improve his vocabulary he had learned a new word every day, and remembered every one of them. Five minutes' conversation with him sent you to the dictionary for the rest of the afternoon. In the scene where the prehistoric animals start to chase us, instead of yelling, 'Run!' he explained in detail *why* we should run away from the enormous carnivorous tyrannosaurus, but we needn't fear the vegetarian brontosaurus (now correctly known as apatosaurus) . . . The animals were not actually on stage in this scene – they would be added later by double exposure – and it didn't really matter if you called them Joe, Gus and Heimie so long as you looked terrified and scarpered. But

With Jocko the monkey, saboteur of scenes, in The Lost World

Bessie Love
First National Star in
"THE LOST WORLD"
and her
"TWISTUM"
BABY DINOSAUR

She writes:

Dear Twistums _

Here I am with your Baby Dinosaur.
It is the cutest thing in the world and
I play with it at the studio. That shows
how I like it, for really it is cunning.
Thanks to you.

Bessie Love

Wally Beery couldn't pass up a chance like this. With the whole company standing round waiting for 'Camera!' he asked Mr Hoyt, 'Does the pterodactyl fly into this scene? No? Then would you just explain it again?' And he would! Poor Mr Hoyt. I'm sure he would laugh now.

Our unit was working on the film for six or eight weeks, and became as close as a family. And when the last shot was taken of the captured apatosaurus escaping down the Thames to the sea and freedom, thereby releasing us to go to other jobs, did we go home? Catch up on sleep? Certainly not! Everybody came to my dressing-room and we sat up the rest of the night complaining about the long working hours, the income tax, our agents, and hilariously reminiscing.

Chapter Nine

TOMMY MEIGHAN, THEN ONE OF the most popular male stars, wired from New York to find if I was free for his next lead – Lasky's had kept telling him I was not available. They didn't know Tommy: in an hour and a half my mother and I were on the train, and I played a full-blood Iroquois in *Tongues Of Flame*.

I hadn't asked the studio for living expenses on location, which was what New York was for me – we still had to keep our flat out home. I loved the East and wanted to stay, but the Biltmore Hotel was not cheap. Then Richard Barthelmess, at that time at the height of his career, asked me about being in *Soul-Fire*.

Dick himself came to interview me at the Biltmore. In my hotel bedroom (with, I should add, the door wide open) he told me the story of the film and acted out the parts, going down on one knee and so on as the plot demanded. I'd never seen Dick before and no agent represented either of us – he just wanted me in his picture, and I said yes.

Everything most serious actors dream of doing, Dick Barthelmess did, thoroughly and successfully. He had a small, tightly-knit, permanent film company of his own; he chose his own director, scenarist, cutter, cameraman, books and plays to be adapted, and the cast. His films were distributed through Inspiration Pictures.

Made in 1925, *Soul-Fire* was the film version of *Great Music*, a Broadway success by Martin Brown. Dick was the star of this sad story of how great music was inspired. I was in the South Sea episode, playing Dick's sarong-clad, Hula-dancing leading lady with a wig like a cobweb shawl down to my waist. I hadn't learnt to do the Hula, so a teacher came to my hotel room and I practised without ceasing; I answered the telephone, ate breakfast, made up and dressed without missing a beat.

Dick's studio sent me to Albert Vargas to have my portrait painted; this was to be used for a magazine cover, and would be good publicity for the

With wings by Albert Vargas

film. Albert Vargas was a Latin American, I think, and very charming. After the initial pleasantries he said casually: 'You can take your things off over there,' and waved towards a screen. Well, I'd already removed my hat, coat and gloves and I didn't have the removal of anything else in mind. However he was so busy with his paints and brushes that I didn't like to disturb him and obviously he meant me to undress. I was quite used to having photographic portraits taken of me wearing very expensive clothes – fur coats, all sorts of hats, dresses with fish-tail trains – but I knew that artists liked to paint their subjects *au naturelle*. Anyway, Mr Vargas was very sweet and I got through the sitting somehow.

I had to come back the next day for another sitting. When I arrived Mr Vargas made most profuse apologies. He had told his fiancée about our picture and his beloved had nearly floored him. 'Do you realize what you've done?' she'd said. 'You'll ruin her career!' He had wondered how he could possibly do that by painting a beautiful picture. His fiancée, however, knew something about films. She pointed out that for any *ingénue* to appear out of a sun-bonnet and hoop skirts spelled disaster, and if he did not want to have me turned out in the street he must *do* something. He did! In the picture the back is still bare and a fair amount of it is showing

96

Without wings photographed by James Abbe

but, if you notice, it has wings! Also, where a glimpse of bust showed before it is now faintly clouded over with flowers whose scent the sprite is enjoying as they rest on her arm and hand (with rather long nails for a fairy, I would say). And the Eton crop which everyone was wearing then has a tiny sprig of a stubborn cowlick which you can see only if you look for it, and which I never did learn to make stay flat.

We worked in the very heart of New York City, in the tiny De Forest studio, which was then engaged in perfecting sound films – I remember vaguely thinking what a silly idea it was. Usually studios in New York, London or Rome are miles out of town but Dick saw to it that he could lean out of his dressing-room window and call a cab by lifting a finger.

The studio was too small to have a canteen, which posed a problem: where to lunch without changing our peculiar make-up and costume so we could get back to work within a normal noon break. This was solved by going to a favourite Italian restaurant of Dick's and eating in the cellar. Room was cleared for a table amid the barrels and crates. Little did the diners upstairs realize that down among the melons there was a whole company, with Dick as a barefoot beachcomber and I in full South Sea Island slap, eating spaghetti and playing the ukelele. While waiting for

97

Above: *on location with Dick Barthelmess for* Soul-Fire. *Below:* B.L. *did the Charleston everywhere including here, on the breakwater on location for* Soul-Fire, *Dick Barthelmess looking on. Noël Coward, among others, credited B.L. with teaching him to Charleston*

lunch the company kept time by clapping their hands for an extra performance of my Hula-dancing up on the table.

Our exterior shots were to be taken in Fort Lauderdale, Florida. With a free day and night off work, Dick, our Publicity man Fred Smith and I set off for Palm Beach in a car loaned to Dick for the publicity. We all three had loads of friends down there for the season. I was taken along on one condition: no pampering. I was to be one of the fellows and fend for myself. Further: the first one to meet friends would leave the others, and no hard feelings. My companions stressed this and glared at me. When we hit Palm Beach I saw a friend at once and left the boys – they were furious.

Not for long, though. I missed my playmates and soon joined them on somebody's houseboat. From there we crashed a party given by another of Dick's friends. This was an extremely formal affair: until you have seen an Italian Palace at Palm Beach, you've never seen anything starched. Though our hostess had never set eyes on Fred or me before, we were Dick's friends – that was enough. She welcomed us in, had her maid sew me into her best Patou number with no back, and we were away! I felt like Cinderella. I didn't look like her, however; she wore glass slippers, while I was wearing my flat brown-and-white sports shoes – what the British call co-respondent's shoes. But no matter. After dancing the night through and eating several meals, I was unstitched and we started back, with me driving. My hostess – and everyone else – made me promise I would get to the wheel first.

After a while, the car began exploding like a veritable Vesuvius. Nothing serious: it had just boiled dry. We stopped at a water tap across the road from a freight train which was getting up steam. Dick started to chuckle down in his collar, skipped lightly across the road and the next thing we knew, he was on top of that live locomotive – they're hot, you know – and was ringing the bell. He looked down at us and grinned triumphantly. 'I've always wanted to do that,' he said.

Our beast watered, the car, Fred and I were ready to go. But no amount of persuasion could get Dick down from his new toy. I pleaded; I joked; I pretended to be angry (maybe I was by then). At last I assured him I was going to drive off; he could come with us or not, as he chose. He laughed. I drove off – and kept on driving into the sunrise until I reached our hotel, with Fred asleep beside me.

My mother was awake, though. She didn't find my cavorting very funny. 'You needn't go to bed,' she said brightly, 'those two young men should be here any time now.' 'What two young men?' I asked wearily. 'Oh, don't you remember? Those boys you thought so attractive? You promised an interview for their Military Academy paper.' 'Oh, no!' I moaned. 'Also,' she chirped, 'Mr Robertson [the director] found a location yesterday and we leave in a few minutes.'

We had come to Fort Lauderdale to photograph the surrounding everglades, swamps, lakes, bayous and rivers. But this was 1925, the year of the Florida boom, and where six months before Dick and the same crew had shot the jungle scenes for *Classmates*, we now found lawns, bungalows and canals. A new location had had to be found – fast – by the distraught director.

Mother now greeted me with the news that the director was no longer distraught and I was about to be wafted to the new labour camp. I just had time for a shower before leaving. Dick and Fred had private transportation – the borrowed car – so they could sleep all day when Dick had returned, by whatever means, and come along when they chose. *I* had to be jostled into a coach with the rest of the company, bouncing over the road.

At last we arrived and unpacked. Very soon Dick and Fred came in. Until then I didn't know if Dick had got back to the hotel or what had happened to him, and I was beginning to squirm. News of our horseplay had got around. No one blamed Dick – they never did. But me? They thought I had two heads. I fully expected that neither the Star nor the Publicity man would ever speak to me again. But no . . . 'You think you're going to bed,' said Dick with what was meant to be a leer. 'Well, you're not,' said Fred, crooking his finger at me. 'You're coming to the Silver Slipper.' I went. Tired? Who, me?

Dick eventually told me how he'd returned. As soon as he realized I was not coming back with his car, he got down from the train and, still tight from the party, went up to a house alongside the railroad, went in, slapped the table and demanded breakfast. The woman there must have recognized him, and found somebody to give him a lift.

For our new location we lived on a houseboat. Besides Dick, there was John Robertson, the director; his wife, scenarist Josephine Lovett; my mother; Harriet Sterling, the actress who played my mother; Fred Smith and myself. The camera crew and the rest of the company stayed on shore.

Anyone who has worked any length of time in films has had his stint of rough locations: no running water – what am I saying! – no *water*, running or otherwise, except what's hauled in. This last location for *Soul-fire* made up for any bad ones I had ever suffered. It was an experience which the uninitiated imagine happens all the time, but in my fairly long career it is the only such experience I've known.

In Miami in the morning, while we were still asleep, the houseboat put out for the island of our location. We had breakfast on board, worked hard, swam – I got so brown I needed no make-up to look like a Polynesian – and went ashore in the evening. Such was work with Richard Barthelmess. He was a good actor and friend. We miss him, but to think of him is to laugh and chuckle, not to cry.

After *Soul-Fire*, still freelancing, I worked for Famous Players-Lasky's. They 'bailed me out' of the Biltmore and sent me home to do a young character lead in *A Son Of His Father* by Zane Grey. Vic Fleming was the director and I got to know him pretty well; he was as big as a bull moose and one of my beaux. (After *A Son Of His Father* had been made I asked him, frankly, why he had agreed to make such a bad film and he asked me, frankly, if I knew how much money the film had made.) Vic went on to make *Gone With The Wind, Joan Of Arc* and many others. *I* went on to *New Brooms*, directed by William de Mille; *The King On Main Street* with Adolphe Menjou, directed by Monta Bell and photographed by Jimmy Wong Howe; and *The Song And Dance Man*, directed by Herbert Brenon, who had just made *Peter Pan*.

Now I was back playing leads again, many of them quite glamorous, for a good salary in good productions, all with the finest casts. In *Lovey Mary* by Alice Hegan Rice, author of *Mrs Wiggs Of The Cabbage Patch*, I was the little girl; that was for M.G.M., with Bill Haines.

Young April, for the Cecil B. De Mille Studio, directed by Donald Crisp, was the most romantic Ruritanian romance, with beautiful clothes by Adrian. In that I played a wealthy young duchess educated in America; in *Going Crooked*, directed by 'Uncle' George Melford for Fox, I was a crook. Dear Kenneth Hawks, my future brother-in-law, was the supervisor.

The story of *Dress Parade*, which I made next, was eventually used in *two* films. The script, set in West Point, the Sandhurst College of America, was first turned down by the Cecil B. De Mille Studio, and was then submitted to M.G.M., who grabbed it. Meantime someone retrieved it from the wastepaper basket at De Mille's and said, 'Looky!' M.G.M. was by now mounting a company to occupy West Point, using that as the name of their film starring Bill Haines and Joan Crawford. So we were smartly set up and set off to make *Dress Parade* there first – with William Boyd (later Hopalong Cassidy), and me as the Academy Superintendent's daughter.

Donald Crisp was directing our effort. He was a clever director and a nice man, but he was also a square. Just as we were leaving for West Point, my cousin Goldie Savage came out from Cincinnati to visit us, and when I mentioned to Donald that Mother would be staying with Cousin Goldie instead of coming with me as usual, he bellowed like a dignified sergeant caught off guard. 'What! Take you to the United States Military Academy without a chaperone!!!!!!! Young lady, you tell your mother to pack. Quick!' So Cousin Goldie held the fort with the chauffeur-chef, housemaid and part-time gardener while Mother and I sallied forth.

It was summer vacation and most of the cadets were away, so we used not only the picture-postcard surroundings, but also the interiors, barracks and mess hall. We even used the chapel, where Bill Boyd, tears gushing, is transformed from a cocky young pug to a nice fellow, earnestly praying to stay on at the Point and not be kicked out as he well deserves.

Not all the cadets – pronounced kaydets – were away, however. I became a kaydet girl and was beaued around, usually by a covey of them, to feed hops and on long strolls through story-book woods and Flirtation Walk.

With summer, cadets wore white uniforms, starched stiff as boards, which they were not allowed to crease. In that get-up they could run, stand still or walk, never sit down. Nor were they allowed to ride in cars at

Left: *in the title role of* Lovey Mary *for M.G.M.* Right: The Song And Dance Man, *with Tom Moore, directed by Herbert Brenon for Famous-Players Lasky*

that time. They had to walk everywhere. So I walked with them – if I'd stayed longer I would soon have had the muscles of a long-distance runner. At the hops we always danced as long as we dared, still allowing time for them to escort me by foot to the Thayer Hotel just outside the post gates, off limits. They could bring me to the steps but not come inside, and then would *run* all the way back to barracks.

No female except the Queen of the Belgians had ever been allowed to eat in the mess hall. I was dying to get in. My gallants put their close-cropped heads together to figure out how it could be done. If they should be – or rather, when they *would* be – caught, they planned most nobly who would do the 'tours' (West Point's usual form of punishment: square-bashing solo in the quadrangle). It was brilliant military strategy, worked out to the last detail. I was so excited I could hardly keep my mind on making the picture. But once I was back at the hotel, away from those gorgeous magnets, I woke up to what a selfish thing I was doing in allowing such an escapade, and I called it off.

When *Dress Parade* was finished I took a tearful goodbye look at my

William Boyd (later Hopalong Cassidy) and B.L., in Dress Parade

champions after our farewell party. They were engrossed in the souvenirs the studio had given each cadet who had worked on the film; sitting inside the coach taking them back to barracks, bright lights behind glass, they neither saw nor heard the outside world . . .

I'd been given souvenirs, too. An autographed copy of *Hope Thou In God* from the composer and choirmaster of the Academy, F. C. Mayer; the tiny Army class pin made by Tiffany's; and I have the usual brass buttons with the Army insignia which all the *femmes* beg off the boys – 'cadets!' – and a 'fried egg', as they call the brass insignia on the front of their caps, which you never see as long as those penetrating eyes are looking at you from under it. I gave it to my grandson last Christmas, for his toy tank.

Rubber Tires in 1927 came next, for the C. B. De Mille Studio again – not an important picture, but great fun; then *The American* (*The Flag Maker*) with Charlie Ray and Ward Crane. This was made for J. Stuart Blackton, using a new invention – a huge camera with stereoscopic lenses. Unlike the usual experimenter, Commodore Blackton didn't expect me to work

Benny Rubin, B.L., Frank Capra, Johnny Walker during filming of The Matinée Idol

for nothing. My salary went up and I started buying a house again.

Then – boom! I was unemployed for eight months.

If, like me, you *still* want to stick it, you start all over again – not at the beginning, of course; by now you're supposed to have learned something. A small picture at the C. B. De Mille lot came along, *A Harp In Hock*, with a nice director, Renaud Hoffman. I had to try to teach Joe Striker to waltz with me.

In Willy Wyler's first non-western feature film – *Anybody Here Seen Kelly?* – I took the character lead, a French girl who comes to New York on the 'invitation' of a flannel-mouthed copper while he's overseas in the First World War; Tom Moore played the flat-foot. You should have seen how we snarled up the cars when, at high noon, with my little bundles and paper bags, I threw my arms round Tom's neck as he directed traffic at 42nd and Broadway.

Sally Of The Scandals came along about then – 1928 – with Allan Forrest, Lottie Pickford's husband, for F.B.O. (which later became R.K.O.). The director was Lynn Shores, who'd been Herbert Brenon's assistant on *The Song And Dance Man* two years before, so he couldn't have been directing long. I nearly cried watching him one night; it was cold, late and raining, and he was hunched over his script figuring out shots still needed before he could call it a day. There's far more to filming than just saying, 'Okay! Let's shoot it!'

The Matinée Idol, with Johnny Walker, was made at Columbia, which was still on Poverty Row. *But* it was directed by Frank Capra. Frank preferred to stay where he could make films the way he wanted, even though the budget was small, without any interference from an assembly-line studio's board of directors and shareholders breathing down his neck.

If, as I did, you run into a gentlemen's agreement among the big boys not to bid against each other while you're freelancing, you may not even realize at first that you are out of work, and think you are only 'resting' between jobs. Unemployment in our profession is, of course, accepted as an occupational hazard; in 1928 it happened yet again, and, as usual, I was unprepared.

This time I went for advice to my lawyer, Edwin J. Loeb. Besides working for a couple of the biggest corporations in California he was also a good friend of mine, and he came up with a practical suggestion. He said that perhaps I was too well known – maybe what people wanted was someone new, someone fresh – and told me to go and see the agent Ivan Kahn, discoverer of new faces. The very fact that Ivan represented anyone meant that he had found someone interesting. It wasn't long before I found out how this gentleman – a retired boxing champion – got places. He used his imagination. He very soon advised me to forget all about the film business and prepare for the stage.

As a matter of fact, after completing *Soul-Fire* with Dick Barthelmess, I'd gone to Cuba for a holiday, and on the ship coming home, Lawrence Schwab, the famous Broadway producer, saw me doing the Rhumba, which I had just learned in Havana and which was to become a wild vogue. Mr Schwab wanted to put me in his next New York show – *Hit The Deck* or *No, No, Nanette!*, one of those.

I'd done the Charleston in a couple of films at Lasky's, and an actress in *The Song And Dance Man* kept urging me to go on the stage and cash in on the fact that I was forever being cast as a musical comedy dancer, my first such part being in *The Midlanders*, for which I was sent to Kosloff's ballet school. Natacha Rambova, future Mrs Rudolph Valentino, was one of my ballet teachers. (I am not implying that I became a ballerina in a fortnight – but since I was playing a 'natural' dancer it was important that I should not fall over when I took off with the birds and the bees in the forest.)

For *The Song And Dance Man*, Lasky's sent me to Murray's dance school for a routine. Following this Herbert Brenon film, I went to Paris and was offered *No, No, Nanette!* by a producer who'd seen me doing the Charleston whenever anyone asked me to, in every nightclub I entered. I couldn't take him seriously – I'd never had stage training, I was just doing it for fun.

But, next thing, Ivan Kahn arranged for me to be in a stage play in San Francisco: *Burlesque*, by Arthur Hopkins and George Manker Watters.

Left: *Treading the boards for the first time: B.L. in the stage play* Burlesque, *with Jere Delaney* Above: *Fanchon & Marco's revue on tour. By the truck are the four Harmony Singers*

Then he signed me for a revue on the West Coast, to learn about the theatre.

The actor's nightmare is to be unemployed for so long that you become forgotten, valueless. Anybody can wear greasepaint; the art is in knowing how to do it and still pay the rent.

On the set of The Broadway Melody: *director Harry Beaumont (centre) handing over all his old megaphones – no use on sound films – to Jack Cummings, left. Between them, Charles King. Anita Page and B.L. hold the historic Sound Stage notice*

Chapter Ten

ALL THE BEST CINEMAS IN the 1920s gave a full hour's live variety show on the programme besides a feature film, news reel and two-reel comedy. Fanchon & Marco presented the live shows in the large cinemas up and down the West coast; and they now built a revue around me.

Sometimes the films on the programme had sound, and often the apparatus would break down and couldn't be moved back to give us room for our set and stairway, which covered the whole stage. Because of the cumbersome speaker, we then had to work in the shallow uncluttered front of the stage, almost in the footlights. When managers who had not yet installed sound equipment asked tentatively what I thought of the new medium, I told them that sound film was a nuisance, a passing fancy: not to give it a thought.

But back in Hollywood M.G.M. had seen the success of Jolson's *The Jazz Singer*, made by Warner's, and were planning their own first sound effort: *The Broadway Melody*, a back-stage story of two sisters in a variety act. I was still on tour with the revue when they began trying to persuade me to leave the show and come home to make a test for it. Ivan suggested that they go see some of my films playing in town at the time to find out how I photographed. He promised them he could get me home if I was offered a contract. But no, a test must first be made.

I'd known every executive in every studio for years. They'd come *to* Hollywood – I'd come *from* it. I felt that if they really wanted me they'd have offered me a contract. So I said, No. I'd had enough Hollywood unemployment along with all the over-employment through the years; working on the stage appealed to me. Our tour was to finish in Salt Lake City – halfway across the United States – and I was heading east . . .

Ivan suggested a compromise: why not come home for an extended week of the tour in Grauman's Egyptian Theatre? The salary was quite

B.L's first Talkie: The Swell Head, *with Eddie Foy, Jr*

beautiful, I could make their test then, and always go on to New York afterwards if they didn't like it. And while we were waiting he arranged with Bryan Foy for me to work opposite Bryan's younger brother, Eddie Junior, in *The Swell Head*, a charming back-stage romance in which I played a dancer. So *The Swell Head*, made at Warner's, was my first Talkie.

M.G.M. did like the test. *The Broadway Melody* had originally been written by Eddie Goulding for the Duncan Sisters – Rosetta, nicknamed Hank, and Vivian, called Queenie in the story; but something went wrong with the negotiations (I knew nothing about this at the time – Rosetta told me about it long afterwards) and in the end I got the part of Hank, the little one, and beautiful Anita Page played Queenie.

Sound was new to all the studios except Warner's. At M.G.M. we would rehearse a dramatic scene and hear the play-back; the sound engineers would say, 'Too much echo' (or not enough something else); and we would vacate the set, which would then be stripped of curtains, furniture, rugs – everything except the walls. Carpenters would swarm on to the set and hammer, hammer, hammer all the floorboards; everything would be replaced on the set, curtains re-hung, thicker carpets laid; we would rehearse again – emotion and all; again hear the play-back, again hear the engineers' 'No!' and again try something different – more curtains, gauze walls. We kept on until it was as near perfect as we could turn it out at that stage, then went on to the next scene. We improved so much as we went along that the end didn't match the beginning.

We used Vitaphone sound at first, which was recorded by a gramophone needle cutting into a large wax disc up in the control room. If you made too sudden or too loud a noise the needle jumped and skipped about, ruining the whole record. The camera was put into a sound-proof booth to eliminate camera noise. Then they got a kind of sleeping garment for it.

This whole caper was new to all of us, and we felt so sorry for our camera assistant, who got dreadfully fussed when he had to prepare the Kodak in its nightie. They were taking this shot from the ceiling of the stage, and every time he fed the camera its film and tucked it up, he always forgot to remove the crank. As soon as the camera was switched on, the crank would begin turning inside the jump-suit and going crazy. Everyone yelled Cut! and this poor fellow, with all M.G.M. watching him from the floor below, unbuttoned the cantankerous machine, changed its innards, then trussed it up again – with the crank still inside – and again pandemonium broke out on 'Camera!' He did this half a dozen times before he could make himself remove that handle before fastening the sound-proof overcoat.

Then we used film which recorded sound alone and had to be married to the visual film, synchronizing action with dialogue (and with aeroplane drones which we hadn't even heard in the studio, causing yet more re-takes). As long as the two films were in 'sync' all was well. But they had only to be one frame out for the result to be hilarious: a fatal explosion and

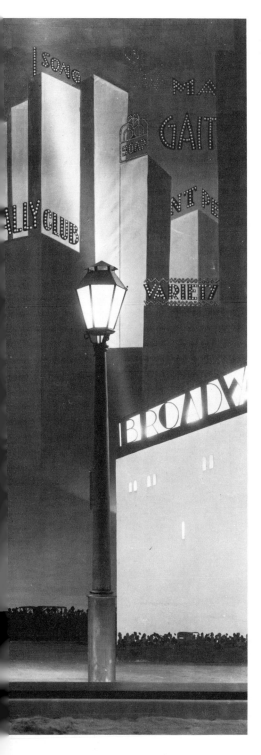

'Queenie' and 'Hank' with Charles King, 'the hoofer in love with us both'

113

Above: The Broadway Melody *on stage, complete with ostrich feathers and chorus line.* Right: *backstage drama: Hank's (B.L.'s) fiancé has fallen in love with her sister Queenie*

the man was dead long before the bang was heard – disastrous to a drama. We would stamp and whistle in the projection room until the operator left his crossword and adjusted the two films in the projector.

Since ours was a musical, we had a big orchestra on the set with us, but out of shot, to accompany the vocals. Soon they started pre-recording the music and songs, so the singers sang and the dancers danced to the play-back of their own music sessions. All stages had been built for silent films and so had to be completely altered – padded with coconut matting or wadding of some sort.

All this made for a long day – ten, twelve or more hours at a stretch, all without overtime payment. Usually press stills are taken when you have a free moment between scenes, but there never *was* a free moment between scenes. I promised to come back one day for their shots after we had finished so that the Exploitation Department could relax. The film completed, I returned to sit for the promised portraits, and, as I left, passed the barber's shop where Irving Thalberg, my boss as well as an old friend, was being spruced up in a huge enveloping barber's gown.

By now I'd bought a one-way ticket to New York, where I wanted to meet Florenz Ziegfeld. I called to Irving, 'Goodbye!'; he called, 'Goodbye!'; I waved my railway ticket and said, 'I'm off to New York' – and he left the barber's chair, gown and all, and came out to me. 'What'd you say?' 'New York. I'm going to New York.' 'When you coming back?' 'I don't know. Maybe I'm not.' 'Come and see me before you leave the studio.' 'Okay.'

And so I was signed up.

My contract was for forty weeks, spread over a year, with options on M.G.M's side for a couple of years or so. But I still went to New York for a holiday, and through Louis Shurr, the agent, I met Mr Ziegfeld, who gave me an audition in his office. He had a piano there, and I'd brought an accompanist. I'd learned a dance routine which I promptly forgot, and had to ad lib; but Mr Ziegfeld seemed pleased. He came out from behind his desk and said some nice things; I would be hearing from him through Mr Shurr. He was just preparing to do *Showgirl*.

A Florenz Ziegfeld production would never hurt any studio's prestige, and I thought M.G.M. might allow me the twelve weeks off at the beginning of my contract instead of at the end, in order to be in the show. But before I could ask permission a telegram arrived from Irving: 'I take for granted that you have already left for the coast'. So that was that. I went dutifully home and Lupe Velez did *Showgirl*, with Eddie Foy, Jr.

Just a word about that forty weeks lark. If you thought you would ever have twelve weeks off at a stretch to go on holiday or work for someone else, you were wrong. Every day that you were not called upon to act – and there are bound to be *some* days, sometimes even a couple of weeks between films – that was your 'free' time. During that period you would be interviewed, photographed, do press stunts, make personal appearances, present trophies, greet visiting firemen, etc., all unpaid. All this activity comes under 'Publicity and Exploitation', and at the end of forty paid weeks you would find that in reality the calendar had chalked up fifty-two.

Although our film had not yet opened anywhere, the Exploitation Department had conditioned prospective audiences with their press blurbs: 'Chorus girls in costumes an ant could drag uphill!', and pictures and interviews in every paper about everything concerning the film. It was an assured success, sold out before it ever hit town.

Before the show, I took some friends to dinner upstairs at the *Montmartre* nearby on Hollywood Boulevard. Blanche Sweet, a very old friend, was one of them. I was anxious to see the film, but first I had to order dinner for my guests. Finally Blanche snapped, 'Oh, for Heaven's sake! Just order some meat and vegetables and show some excitement over your opening night!'

The Broadway Melody had its 'world première' with all the trimmings in Grauman's Hollywood Chinese Theatre on 1 February, 1929. Long before the performance huge, grotesque searchlights panned the sky, mutely demanding attention. Powerful arc-lights flooded the forecourt banked solid with delighted fans. Cameras everywhere, microphones, loudspeakers and screams of recognition as favourites from every studio alighted from their shiny black limousines, calling 'hello, everybody' over the mike, accepting wild applause and making the slow advance along the red carpet to the theatre entrance. If any actor is self-conscious about this part of his performance, he shouldn't be. It's part of his job.

But what really is exciting is what happens inside the theatre on that opening night. For one thing, the place is packed to the gunwales with your workmates, and theirs is a special kind of praise. Those who share the donkey work that goes into *any* production, good or bad – the author, producer, director, assistants, actors, cutter, cameramen, art department, and crew of electricians, carpenters, paperhangers – *any*body who has actually sweated it out on the floor – they are the ones who know if you are a phoney.

And when the picture turns out to be good – just right – the way you meant it to be – and this elephantine cinema in 'the town where they made 'em' comes to life from cellar to rafters with everyone applauding and shouting their appreciation – 'Oh boy! Attagirl!' – in the middle of the film, it is something. I tell you, it really is.

With the great success of *The Broadway Melody* M.G.M. had overnight changed their output from Silent to Sound production of films. They followed it up with *The Hollywood Revue Of 1929*, whose cast list reads like a Who's Who in Hollywood. Every actor was under contract to the studio, and they were all stars, or had been and were now supporting players – like Marie Dressler who soon, after many years away from studios, would become a film star again, and on the same lot, in *Tug Boat Annie* and *Min And Bill* with Wally Beery.

In our revue, Marie Dressler burlesques Cleopatra, singing 'I'm The

Marie Dressler, B.L. and Polly Moran in their 'I'm Marie – I'm Polly – I'm Bess' number in The Hollywood Revue of 1929

Queen'; Laurel and Hardy throw pies at each other, Babe Hardy finally falling face down in a cream cake big enough to take care of their antics for some time; Buster Keaton does a 'Dance of the Seven Veils' à la Cooch, but deadpan; Polly Moran sends up 'Your Mother and Mine' after it has been sung straight by Charlie King; Conrad Nagel was very popular at the time, but who knew he could sing? Yet you couldn't have asked for dulcet-er tones than he renders in 'You Were Meant for Me', sung to Anita Page; Joan Crawford, who had been a dancer in her pre-Hollywood days, does a number; so does Marion Davies, with nine thousand cadets in West Point uniforms.

Then Marie, Polly and I – 'I'm Marie, I'm Polly, I'm Bess' – clad in toddlers' rompers, do a 'poop-poop-a-doop' take-off of the Brock Sisters' close harmony singing in the show, and Ukelele Ike (Cliff Edwards), Charlie King and Gus Edwards complete our sextet for 'Strolling in the Park One Day', in Floradora costume, which by trick photography must be the fastest strip-change on record. Throughout, Jack Benny and Bill

Haines do a two-handed compering of the show, Jack making unhelpful explanations about each act as he introduces it.

One of the first, if not the very first, strikes in the film industry was taking place at that time. As yet we had no Screen Actors' Guild and American Equity, the 'straight' actors' union, was hoping to establish one. They forgot one thing: strike action does not affect contract players, and almost all the well-known ones were then under contract to some studio. The only people able to refuse employment were a small handful of freelance players – Lois Wilson was one, Jetta Goudal was another – and the little dancers, male and female, who were always engaged by the picture anyway. The studio couldn't have cared less. It was no trouble to find pretty girls out home and they could all dance: someone just went to the beach, bellowed, and all the swimmers came dancing in.

However, there were no male dancers around – none with experience. So very quickly a line of those had to be found, for one thing, for me. Because I was doing another little number for *The Hollywood Revue Of 1929*.

Harry Rapf, an old hand with vaudeville from way back, was supervising the film and called me into the office to say that they'd come up with the idea that everybody should do something to surprise, something an audience had never seen them do – or, better still, something they had never attempted before. At which point he asked, 'Have you ever done an acrobatic dance?' I was so startled that I didn't have time to get out of it. 'Why, no,' I stammered. 'Fine. That takes care of you,' he said. 'Go see Sammy Lee.' Sammy was the choreographer.

Well, I've always wanted to learn acrobatics – how to fall, and all that. Down at the beach I once asked Keaton to teach me. He said, 'Let me see your wrists,' took one look, laughed and pushed me away.

Weak wrists or no, I'd seen one of the pretty routines Sammy Lee was dreaming up while I was in New York. It's pretty if performed by a good solo dancer supported by many strong, clever male choristers who rehearse for weeks until they work together like a team. You take two lines of them, facing each other and holding out their hands. Then you, with your feet held firmly by the centre of the line, relax (!) back on the hands of half the line-up, whence you are flipped up, twisted in mid-air, and allowed to land on the other half of the line of outstretched hands waiting to catch you (theoretically).

Doing this a couple of dozen times, non-stop, can be very effective seen from the front – and also, felt from the rear. These bright young men had never set eyes on each other before they took me by the heels to swing me back and forth like the handle of a fan opening and closing. The first time we tried it, on 'hup!', both sides – they must have thought I was suddenly going to put on weight – all gave one mighty heave and I went sailing out over everybody's head, landing on the backs of my heels in another part of the studio.

We tried again. The same thing happened, only this time I sailed away the other side. Once more, and I dropped straight through their arms on to the hard floor . . . And this was only one out of many acrobatic routines. After each session I'd go to the studio osteopath to have things snapped back into place and my legs levelled up. I spent as much time with him as I did with Sammy and the boys.

Then someone had the bright idea of letting the boys learn the routine first, and practise throwing around a real acrobat. Which they did – the little ballet dancer, daughter of one of the electricians, who danced on point in 'Wedding of the Painted Doll' in *The Broadway Melody*. When we came to shoot it, I was trussed up with adhesive tape like a football player to ensure that I remained in one piece. My glamorous costume was slipped over the top, and all protective taping which showed down the front and most of the back was cut away. Thus I did the number called, 'I Never Knew That I Could Do A Thing Like That'.

Jack Benny thought up the introduction to my number. He said, 'She's so little, why can't I take her out of my pocket? You can do that in pictures, can't you?' He was intrigued with the potential of film – trick shots which make people little or enormous, or cut them in half. He thought of more ideas: after he had taken me out of his pocket I was to stand on his hand and talk to him in a squeaky voice until he set me down and I 'grew up'. The studio agreed – it was a wow! But what Jack didn't know was that trick photography, always time-consuming, is therefore done after everything else has been shot, while the bridging music is being written. This was Jack's first film, and he had no notion how long things take; he had been a vaudeville headliner for years and had just taken a few weeks off to do our revue, after which he was to continue his tour from San Francisco.

We started making *Hollywood Revue*, and we went on and on making it. Every once in a while Jack would approach the director, Chuck Reisner, and tentatively inquire in his 'helpless' way, 'You won't forget that shot of me taking Bessie out of my pocket?' 'Oh no, Jack. You see . . .' and Chuck would launch into a technical explanation of how it was to be done. The whole stage had to be completely shrouded in black velvet. My tiny figure, the height of a thimble, standing on his hand, was a trick shot, naturally. Then a dolly track had to be laid the full length of the stage so that in the distance I would look tiny, and as the camera approached me I would appear to grow. Jack listened, mesmerized, the first time he was told all this. The next time he still wanted to hear it – well, yes, he'd been told how it worked, but it was still magic. After the third, fourth and fifth times he suggested, 'Why not just let her wave hello?'

At the end of several weeks' shooting and the final 'Okay!' Jack simply disappeared. He left so fast he could have taken off on his own coat-tails as, still in dress-suit and make-up, he boarded the Lark flyer for San Francisco.

William de Mille, brother of Cecil B. De Mille (they spelt it differently), had been a director for years at Lasky's. I remember passing him on the lot one day. 'Hello,' I said, 'how are you?' His tired face turned towards me. 'With picture,' he sighed. Later he came to M.G.M. while I was under contract there. Lasky's had just finished his last picture without him, after he'd left. I knew he'd just seen it and before I could stop myself I asked what they'd done to it. 'They raped it,' he informed me.

William de Mille was the soul of quiet, retiring dignity, classic wit and good taste. He always wore a battered old hat on the set – he wore it when he went fishing too. He had worn it in 1925 when he made *New Brooms* at Lasky's with Neil Hamilton, Phyllis Haver and me; and now, in 1929, he was still wearing it for *The Idle Rich* at M.G.M.

The Idle Rich was adapted by Clara Beranger from Ruth Ellis's *White Collars*, which had played for years at the little Egan Theatre, Los Angeles, and in New York. It was a delightful comedy, although the lines of the rich executive (played by that heartbreaker Conrad Nagel) would sound awfully pompous now. Today, even the most devoted secretary would tell him to go jump in the lake instead of being carried off to the altar as Leila Hyams was. After the honeymoon she insists that they live with her family in their already overcrowded apartment, so he can see how wonderful they are to have stuck it for so long. She hasn't figured on Cousin Henry, whose persuasive soap-box oratory influences the bridegroom to give away his fortune by building and staffing a hospital for the great Middle Class. ('Rich are all right; poor are taken care of; white collar workers with dignity and low salaries have no champion!' I think now the author had a point there – though I doubt if I understood it in 1929, before the Great Depression had become a fact). James Neill and Edythe Chapman – who were husband and wife in real life – played the father and mother. Experienced, sweet people, they were always playing husband and wife at Lasky's, where they had worked with the Mille brothers, both de and De. Indeed, the Neill Company, starring Edythe Chapman and James Neill, had been the resident rep. at the California Theatre, San Francisco, before 1900.

I doubt if I was any younger than Leila, but I played her young sister, a gum-chewing, wisecracking typist. When first I was told about my part, Mr de Mille told me to take the script home and put my dialogue into my own words, using slang and modern expressions. Making fast tracks to the best gag writer in the studio, Hoppy Hopkins, I gave him the script and begged him to go through it and put in some of his priceless wisecracks. He must not breathe a word about this to anyone, especially my director.

Next day, 'my director' called me over and said casually that Hoppy had been to see him, saying that I had requested him to 'brighten up' the script here and there. He said that he had thanked Hoppy but thought that Miss Beranger (Mr de Mille's wife) had made a good job of the script . . . he added that all he wanted for the scenario was some current flapper slang, which he thought I could ably supply. I still don't know whether I had under-rated or over-rated myself.

The play has its serious moments. The teenage typist's reaction to the news that her millionaire brother-in-law is now a self-made pauper is

120

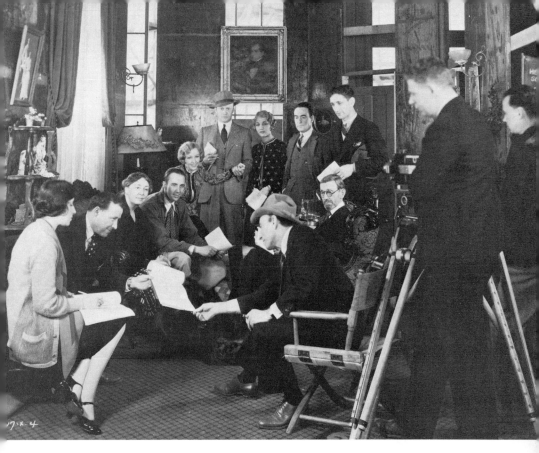

William de Mille (seated, centre) in his famous hat, with the cast of The Idle Rich

heartrending. She tearfully points out that whether he is rich or poor, her educated sister will always have a cultured, respected husband, while she, the younger, flashy, noisy one, uneducated and now without opportunity, has the prospect of a monosyllabic truck driver for a mate, and a life that goes with such an alliance.

Any actress is supposed to shed very wet tears on command – I was once talking to Bebe Daniels on the set as they lit it for her next shot, when suddenly tears started trickling down her face. 'Good heavens!' I thought, 'What have I said?' Someone called, 'Okay, Bebe!', she walked over, did her emotional scene, came back and we finished our conversation. But could I cry for my scene? No.

I know I should have done it, but Mr de Mille wasn't much help, really. For one thing, I don't imagine he'd ever had much truck with tantrums. His attitude towards life always appeared to be sophisticated, urbane, in complete control, a bit cynical: he was a walking understatement. He was expert at exposing superficial, shallow human failings and foibles. But when it came to digging deep into an actor's emotional vitals and dragging out his innermost hidden thoughts, I'm sure William de Mille would have been most embarrassed at the very idea.

I tried to think of all the horrible catastrophes I could to make myself cry. Nothing happened. Mr de Mille tried to 'help' by saying various things, which I listened to instead of concentrating. Then he said, 'Just think of that audience of millions of people out there watching you – watching and waiting all over the world.' Oh-h-h-h! I curled up inside like a worm tapped with a twig. The tears dried up, scared to death, and I found myself imagining 1,000,000 people watching me do a scene in M.G.M's enormous studio in Culver City, instead of imagining myself an insignificant teenager leading off at my family in our clean shabby little kitchen in New York City.

All Mr de Mille's comedy was perfectly timed. He had every camera angle literally drawn in his script before we ever set foot on the stage. He directed the exact moment at which you would crook your finger, before, after or during a line; and we would rehearse or re-take the scene until your finger crooked at his order. One day Miss Beranger, who wrote all his scripts, confided that she had once accused him of ruining his comedy by making it too set and lacking spontaneity. She laughed as she recalled this, because his films were considered by intellectuals to be among the most impeccable to come out of Hollywood. I thought then that she had been right: that he did restrict his actors. Now I think differently. William de Mille's style was not the naturalistic acting I was used to, but the classical comedy of manners, demanding the utmost discipline, and timing was its most important tool.

While we were making *The Idle Rich*, M.G.M. were showing *The Broadway Melody*, still at Grauman's Chinese Theatre, and every night someone from the studio would appear on stage, just to clown or do something. (No one got paid for it.) Many of our gag-writers, serious writers, directors and stars had come from the theatre, especially vaudeville, so a live audience was no problem to them. I was asked to appear so often I felt the theatre should be paying me instead of the studio. I don't believe I have ever seen the ending of *The Broadway Melody* – I've always had to be ready in the wings to go on as soon as it was over.

So one day I asked Mr de Mille for a curtain speech. And Mr de Mille gave me one. Though not in these words, he suggested I say how fortunate I was to have been in such a production, made by such a good company. The effort, ability and thoroughness of many gifted people had made the film a resounding success and I was glad to have been associated with it.

This set me back a little, because I'd never felt anything of the kind. I considered I'd done a darned good job and I was more than pleased to be patted on the back for it. I'd never got such a pat from the studio – I still don't know if they liked it or not. When an audience applauded at the end of the film, to my mind they showed good judgement.

122

However, I had asked the Master for a speech and the Master had given me one. It seemed ungracious (or stupid) not to use it. When the night came, I did say what he'd told me to say, and by the time I was saying it, I meant every word. I'd thought about it a great deal, and I could speak his lines with conviction, because by then I saw that they were true.

At M.G.M., early 1930s

Chapter Eleven

I MARRIED WILLIAM BALLINGER Hawks on 27 December, 1929. And a very white wedding it was. I'd had lots of beaux, who are still my friends (the ones who are still around), but I had no intention of getting married more than once, so I planned to enjoy the proceedings to the full.

I had known Bill's brothers, Howard and Kenneth, long before I met the groom. Edna Purviance, Charlie Chaplin's leading lady, had introduced Bill and me on the Santa Fé express returning to Hollywood from New York. Edna came through the train to my compartment and said she thought I knew the Hawks boys. Yes, I said, I knew the whole family. All, she said, except the youngest: would I like to meet him? *Would* I? I said. Show me! And all the way to Pasadena – for three days – he and I sang 'Moonlight and Roses'. It became our theme song. Often, when he came home to Pasadena for holidays, we would meet. By then Kenneth was married to Mary Astor. When Bill moved back to California, the four of us became inseparable.

I was under contract to M.G.M. when we married. Early on, Howard Strickling, head of Publicity, gave me some sound advice. It's not very much trouble, he said, to respect certain forms of etiquette towards the press, however private a wedding might be. And police, for instance, could ensure that the bride – the groom too, for that matter – could get into the building in order to take part in the service at all, and could prevent the bride being denuded on the front steps by fans seeking swatches of bridal gown as mementoes. Howard Strickling did me proud. He included a motorcycle escort.

When it came to choosing a best man, we loved both Bill's brothers and couldn't decide which one should back him up and catch him if he fainted. We discovered that it was permissible to have both, so we finally had not one best man, but two.

B.L's wedding to William Ballinger Hawks. From left: Norma Shearer, Irene Mayer, Bebe Daniels, Athole Shearer Hawks, Bill Hawks, B.L., Blanche Sweet, Carmel Myers, Edith Mayer Goetz

Afterwards we had a reception at the Ambassador Hotel a few rooms away from Abe Frank's Coconut Grove, where we were all used to dancing to Abe Lyman's band. Many of our guests had arranged their own supper parties to be held there later that night and everyone in the place was dancing and eating with each other before the night was out. As I stood in line to receive guests, my chum Floren Levitt from L.A. High, along with the whole family, whispered in my ear, 'Mazeltov!' and I knew I was really married. Irving Thalberg was our head usher; Blanche Sweet, matron of honour. Bridesmaids were the two Mayer girls, Edith and Irene; Carmel Myers; Norma Shearer (Mrs Irving Thalberg); her sister Athole, now my sister-in-law (Howard's wife); and Mary Astor, also now my sister-in-law (Kenneth's wife). Mary was in a play at the Majestic in town, so she had to join us after the wedding ceremony.

One week later Kenneth was killed in a flying accident. He was directing Warner Baxter in *Such Men Are Dangerous* (his first director's job) for Fox. Howard had been at the airfield seeing him off. Ken asked him to come along for the ride. Howard had one foot on the step, hesitated, then decided not to.

One plane was carrying the actors' doubles; the 'dangerous' man of the title was to·parachute out and pretend suicide. Kenneth and the camera crew were in another plane. The two collided over the ocean. There was a third plane, which flew back for help. That's how we knew where to look for them. No one was saved.

At my hillside home, where Mother still lived, we had put out all our wedding presents, planning a cocktail party to show them off. Bill's mother was there when we heard the news. My mother said she'd never seen such courage as Mrs Hawks showed. There were no tears; she simply refused to give up hope until they actually found Ken's body, and the others, some time later.

During the evening my father rang us from the small Hollywood hotel where he was the night clerk. The pilot of the third plane lived there, and came to the phone. There wasn't much he could tell us: he said probably the two pilots had been blinded by the late straight rays of the sun. Strange, but it was comforting to talk to someone who'd actually been there when it happened.

That day Mary Astor had a matinée. They kept the news from her until after the curtain fell. Now she understood why she'd heard Kenneth call her as she waited in the dressing-room . . . She never went back to their house.

A couple of years after we were married, at the end of my M.G.M. contract, I agreed to do eight weeks in a most gorgeous variety act. M.G.M. allowed us to use clips from *The Broadway Melody*, *Chasing Rainbows* and *The Hollywood Revue*. This build-up on the sound screen was followed by a scene we had made at the R.K.O. studio, of me coming on to a stage and talking into the camera to the audience. Soon a spotlight picked up the live me on the stage in the same dress – a beauty, which had been worn by Joan Crawford for M.G.M. The screen me introduced the stage me to the audience and I carried on a conversation with myself. When the film B.L. got a little flip I threatened to fade her out, signalled to the film operator up in the booth to do so, then I went on with the act. This gag had been done only once before, by a comic – Ted Healey – who had pulled out a gun on-stage and shot himself on screen.

For costumes I had the original *Broadway Melody* one – black sequins, fishnet tights and rhinestone outline of a top hat – and another little red chiffon number the size of a couple of postage stamps with a red feather head-dress three feet high and wide.

The best thing of all in the production was my accompanist, Ted Snyder. All the bands in all the theatres knew and respected him: a kinder and more generous man never existed. While I changed costumes, he played his hit songs, and everybody in the audience, of whatever age, knew all of them.

After I'd signed up for this tour to stomp and Charleston my way across the United States, I discovered that someone would soon have to start making tiny garments. We wanted to shout the news to the world, but thought it wise to keep it a secret for the tour at least. I didn't even tell Ted Snyder; I knew he'd worry about me, and anyway it wouldn't have been the best publicity for a tights-and-spangles performance. But we did send word to my in-laws, who were travelling in Europe, making them swear

Above: See America Thirst,
*with Harry Langdon (left) and Slim
Summerville. Before going into films
Harry Langdon had been a
cartoonist, and created a wide-eyed,
childlike character identical with the
one he played on stage and screen*
Right: *B.L. being 'helped' out of the
window by Gus Shy in* Good
News, *1930, supervised by Bernie
Hyman*

secrecy. Delighted, they cabled back – no signature, just: Grandparents!

In Brooklyn the show played in the big Keith-Albee theatre. We were on their circuit, and although we were strictly variety – no two acts working together – the acts travelled together as a road show, and got to know each other well. Brooklyn is a tough date unless you are either a blues singer or a blue comic out to maim your straight-man. Although the house was full and everyone worked twice as hard as usual we got exactly nowhere. There was an act on just before me, very fast, very funny, which reduced the stage to a shambles every night; no one in the audience ever laughed.

Then one night, when the straight-man ripped off the slap-stick comic's trousers to reveal the long red drawers underneath, there was a roar from the house like a hundred jets breaking the sound barrier. That audience bellowed and bellowed. Every act on the bill absolutely fell on to the stage – half made-up, half-dressed – to find out what had made that audience laugh so hard. We fired questions at the little comic: 'What did you do?' 'What happened?' 'What was it?' He seemed quite dazed and bewildered. At last he said simply, 'I forgot to put them on – the under-pants.'

My 'condition' was one of the best kept secrets in Hollywood. But one of the first telephone calls I got on reaching home after the tour was a reporter who started, 'I understand the stork . . .' 'Yes,' I hollered, 'Yes, yes, YES!' I was so glad to be able to talk about it at last. Girlfriends began ringing up to say, 'Don't buy such-and-such. They cost the earth. I'll loan you mine – but I want it back, don't forget.' Many friends wanted to give baby showers – present-giving parties. I refused all but one: Joan Bennett was a dear friend to us both, and invited all my girlfriends, while Frances Marion gave a similar do for the husbands and beaux.

Joan has always been of a sensible frame of mind. By the time our husbands arrived to take us all home she had seen to it that the presents were also ready to go – a great heap of them, including a large and lifelike model stork.

My Bill had flu and wanted nothing more than to get home and to bed. 'Thanks, Joan,' he said, 'but I'll pick up the presents tomorrow.' Oh no, we weren't having that! Very quickly everything was stowed in our two-seater. We found room for me and my personal burden in the car, but the stork had to perch over the loot in the boot, flapping its wings as we drove down Hollywood Boulevard. I must have had a hunch something was going to happen because that night I slept soundly in the Good Samaritan Hospital. Bill slept there too, not so soundly, on a wooden bench in the waiting room. And the next day Patricia was with us.

We had decided on Patricia if it was a girl: Patty for when she was a baby; Pat for when she went to school; Patricia for when she was grown and having her own family. Her friends have always called her Patsy.

Fade out . . . fade in . . .

Well, things didn't quite turn out the way we'd planned. So in 1935, when Patty was three, I came to London with her and my mother, and stayed on after my divorce. It was not such a bold move as one might think. Six months before, Bill and I had been here on a business holiday, meeting his clients and seeing the plays they were in. Bill was just getting into his stride as a theatrical agent out home; he and his partner (George Volk) represented an important London agency, O'Bryen, Linnet and Dunfee, who looked after the biggest British theatre and film stars. We saw them all when they came out to Hollywood; indeed, some of our closest friends were among the resident British 'colony'. Had Patty been a boy she would have been named Kenneth Ronald after Ronald Colman, a devoted friend to both Bill and me and Bill's first client.

By the time I moved to London people were getting to travel more, and I saw my Hollywood friends here almost more than I had at home. They were always popping in on their way to or from the Continent. Mother stayed for a couple of years, took a good look at another November fog, said, 'California, here I come' and skedaddled.

I was fortunate in the English people I met then. Their thoughtfulness made me see England through a golden glow, and this has never left me (though of course I had to get used to some friends wearing the 'old school tie' so tight that they couldn't bend their necks). I had rented a great, empty flat and arranged to have all my furniture – some antique – sent here from a nine-room house out home. When we discovered that no action whatsoever had been taken about sending it the old-school-tie brigade fell to, and before I knew what had hit me I was up to my knees in beds, tables, chairs and tea-cosies.

In 1938 I was understudying the lead in *The Women* at the Lyric Theatre, and also taking courses in how to care for babies and small children under rough conditions so that I would not be separated from Pat if London was evacuated. The poor officials at the American embassy were going crazy over me: war was as imminent as the rising of the sun, and they were responsible for all their nationals, continually loading up the 'last ship' to the States – there was even a wealthy Anglo-American organization which would pay your fare. Each time I was rung up to be coaxed to go home I always asked where they would suggest I go, since I had no address at home any more. I lived in London now, and expected to go on living here.

Everyone was jittery. Bombs had been expected in London at any minute. One of my closest friends phoned to know if I'd got Pat out of town (Pat was six then). He was appalled when I said, 'No', and told me to pack bedding, bring all the food I could lay my hands on, and come down to the country at once. I had just packed to go when Bill cabled us to return home until at least the governments had made up their minds what was happening.

We didn't stay long. We came back to a country almost at war but, as it were, not wired for sound – the 'phoney war', everyone called it. I helped to evacuate many children and oh, so many pregnant mothers when *all* main roads led *out* of London. Nothing was allowed in until the evacuation of a couple of million children was completed – and no accidents!

America was still neutral, and while able to supply all the 'tools' needed for Britain's war, bent over backwards to keep any American nationals from doing anything to jeopardize that neutrality. I felt guilty about all the allied armies, navies and aircraft keeping us safe and warships convoying our food supplies while I was doing nothing to help. I did my best to join up as something – anything. I never had such a welcome in my life as when I applied to be an ambulance driver. They almost burst into tears. 'You are not American! You're Canadian!' 'No. American.' 'Australian?' With everybody nodding, 'Yes', I persisted: 'No. American.' 'You *sound* like a Canadian.' 'I come from Hollywood,' I said. I did not become an ambulance driver. Nor did I help with the air raid wardens. In the local barricaded gas-proof shelter I saw great stacks of blankets waiting for delivery, and boxes of provisions. My little Ford was waiting outside. The warden, in the middle of talking down the phone, was sorry, but 'It's no use – I'd love to – we need help very badly – you're very kind to offer but we simply cannot use Americans . . .' I shouldered my bag and left.

Then a friend had a brilliant idea: she suggested the American Red Cross (nothing to do with nursing). Their entertainment H.Q., unknown to me, had taken over the empty building next door to our empty building. (All our leases had expired about this time and instead of renewing them everyone left town. We lived throughout the war in this big empty block of flats except for one other family and the caretaker.) My Red Cross job was to entertain the G.I.'s confined to hospital wards, and my ukelele was played until it collapsed.

Meantime practising my profession was impossible. All theatres were closed by order, and when the London ones re-opened the 'doodle bugs' immediately blasted them shut again.

I went out to Ealing Studios to see Michael Balcon – Sir Michael, as he is now. 'We're only doing documentary films and epics,' he said. They were just about to launch into a whopper: *San Demetrio, London,* a true story about the Merchant Navy. An oil tanker catches fire, the crew have to abandon her. After many days in an open boat they sight a ship and row for it – the Demetrio, still afloat and burning. They re-board, douse the blaze and repair her engines enough to bring her into port.

I already knew Sir Michael. I told him then, 'Look! I've got to go to work or go crackers. So will you please find me something. I don't care what it is – if there's nothing for an actress, then any beginner's job on production.' He leaned across his desk and said, 'We need someone to help a new continuity girl. If you don't know something about making pictures now, you never will.'

Sir Michael's manner is brisk and businesslike. In between calling a lot of people on the inter-com, he fired questions at me faster than I could answer them. 'Can you do shorthand?' 'No, but ——' 'Can you type?' 'Yes, but——' 'You'll be screamed at.' 'Okay, if——' 'Work like a horse.' 'Yes ——' 'Join a trade union.' 'Yep!' 'And get paid five pounds a week.' 'You mean I'll get paid?'

Next, in answer to his calls, people began appearing from the various departments which my employment would affect. Sir Michael told them the news: 'I think she's crazy,' he said, 'but we'll see.' They knew I'd been in pictures all my life and we all laughed at my wanting a beginner's job – all of us except the director, Charles Frend. Mr Frend had a sparkling sense of humour – when you knew him, that is. But he was most serious concerning his work, and he and Bob Hamer had spent a year and a half writing *San Demetrio*.

Mr Frend hadn't caught my name. He drew me aside and asked, 'How much experience have you had in films?' 'Oh, all my life.' 'And on continuity? How many scripts have you done?' 'None, that's just the idea.' Gradually he was beginning to understand that I was going to learn on his picture. Hal Mason, studio manager, broke in, 'She's willing to be fired in a fortnight.' After meditating for a bit, Mr Frend said, 'All the sets are being built on huge rockers – to give a boat effect.' 'Is that so?' (I really said that. I heard myself say it.) He continued grimly, 'For matching close-ups to long shots, you can watch the action and tell what was happening each time the rockers changed motion.' 'You mean like, down on the port side when Harry cocked his hat?' It was a deal.

To work on the staff I had to be a union member. It was difficult for me to join the Association of Cine-Technicians because I not only had been an actress, but with any luck would be again, if I could just hold out. Had it been peace time, with ordinary beginners around to fill my shoes, I would never have been allowed to fill theirs. But at last they decided on a War Emergency rating for me, and I was in.

I travelled to the studio on a workmen's ticket every morning: before 7.30 you could travel half-fare. And I came home when the moon was well up. That was my own choosing – actually, work stopped at six o'clock. I stayed on in the prop room, locked in, after everyone had left, typing out my own ideas of whether I was coming or going in the day's work.

I took shorthand lessons at night and on Sundays, and on Saturday afternoons when we didn't work. (Think of not working some afternoon just because it's Saturday. Oh! This wonderful country!) Needless to say, I went around with a shorthand notebook most of the time in order to cram between whiles. The first day I was on the set, a neat man with a precise moustache came on looking for Mr Frend. I knew part of my job would be to take messages and opened my notebook to write down his name. He misunderstood. He was Mr Zorn, the studio lawyer. The minute he saw that book flick open, he stuck his thumbs into his waistcoat armholes and started striding up and down the stage, dictating a most particular business letter to this most exacting director.

It strikes me as funny now but I didn't laugh much at the time. The letter contained a great deal about a nice legal point. It seems that Mr Zorn's own brother had been in the office 'at the time'. That was most important – he had me say it twice, and shook a forefinger menacingly. And 'the car and all papers pertaining thereto would be delivered in due course ——' Or was it 'to be taken away'? I didn't quite catch that bit. I was still writing down about his brother. And I was still writing long after the gentleman had left, inserting here and crossing out there. The plainer I tried to make it, the more muddled I became. Then I made a brilliant decision. When Mr Frend came back on to the set, I just glanced at my notebook and told him that a gentleman had been to see him and would be back.

Actually, I didn't do too badly at that speedwriting – I got up to about sixty-five words a minute, which isn't bad for a raw beginner. Unfortunately you have to be able to read it back, too. And talk about 'rockers' . . . every set in that picture was a boat. I never knew there were so many different kinds. There was a battleship; a cruiser; a tanker; a tug; an open boat with and without sails. When were they up? When down? When on the starboard tack, when on the port? Who was at the sweep? Or was it the tiller? Where did all sixteen men sit? And when did they change places? What were they wearing? Was it buttoned or unbuttoned? How many buttons? Which way was the sea running? *Which way?* It *couldn't* have been! It *was?* Re-take the whole sequence! The sea must run bows to stern. Naturally the boat can't sail backwards!!

Well, I thought I'd been in pictures, but I found I'd never properly been inside the gate. I made a dear friend in the studio, Titch, our boom man (sound man handling the mike on the set). He was a little cockney, tough as they come, and he looked after me as he would his own brother. He proposed me to the union and always told me how much overtime to expect. He made me collect my 'dirty money' – extra pay for unusually dirty work: we had the whole stage ablaze for weeks, and went around as black as the ace of spades.

The first day in any studio anyone feels green and out of place. You wonder what you're doing there anyway, among so many people who all know each other so well. But a sandy-haired electrician made me feel at home right away by saying, 'Good morning, Bright Eyes!' After that he never called me anything else. Titch called me Peach Blossom and Desert Flower. Love, Betty and Betsy are obvious variations; the tea lady got it into her head that they said Patsy, and she could never remember anything else. And Bluey, the big Australian assistant, always hollered, 'Hey! Butch!'

The film took longer to make than we'd figured; and in the middle of it Madge, the continuity girl, was about to have her baby. She had been perfectly wonderful, climbing down on to the set-up from the roof, outside, when the scenes were shot from the ceiling of the stage, and sliding along the stage floor through tons of water being spilt from colossal hoppers overhead. Madge's husband told me one morning about his

134

Wartime in London: B.L. with ration book at the local butcher's

decision for her to stay at home. I knew he would feel happier about her, but I wondered why he was so concerned about me. Then it hit me. That meant I was no longer 'helping' the continuity girl. I *was* the continuity girl – and I was on my own.

Wouldn't Charles Frend come on to the set with fire in his eye and say they were going to re-take everything that'd been shot from a certain angle, to get a more lurid storm effect on the sky backing! Had he only noticed, a close-up of my face would have done just as well. For two days they stopped only long enough between shots for the actors to make proper changes in wardrobe and make the wind and rain heavy enough. Everything they did, said and wore had to be matched to scenes following and preceding. Naturally the weather had to be matched, too, and positions of the wind machines for direction and speed of wind, waves, smoke, fire and spray.

After two days, they had someone 'helping' me. I had to wear suspenders – braces as they say over here – to keep up my slacks at all. I was about as fat as a snake. The company went home to beer and skittles when work was finished, but me – I got to know the night crew better than our own outfit.

When the picture was over I went timidly into the office to see what I would do next. I thought I was leading with my chin but, much to my surprise, I'd been there six months and rated a week's holiday. With pay! I took it too, with my daughter. We went to Scotland: first holiday we'd had since the war began. And of course I picked a fishing village. We stayed with some fisher folk, and the son, who was on leave from the Merchant Navy, knew the old Demetrio. Our room overlooked a toy bay with breezes and storms and everything, just like our re-takes. I enjoyed watching those boats come in, taking a lot of trouble to forget what was happening and who was where when the rock of the boat changed from port to starboard.

I wasn't with the studio much longer. I knew everybody in the place and really wanted to stay, but I had to get back to my own job of acting . . .

What have I done since the war? Oh, I've never stopped in all that time. I'm always doing plays on radio, television, or stage, straight or musical, with long or short tours before or after the London theatre run. Immediately after the war I joined the Lunts at the Lyric in *Love In Idleness*, which they were about to take to entertain the American troops in Germany. General Patton was a personal friend of the Lunts, who stipulated they wanted to play to the G.I.'s in the 'sticks'. A month after peace was declared we opened at the Sarah Bernhardt in Paris – not exactly the provinces, though it was a wise decision to play there – we were packed out for a fortnight.

Following that I played the senator's wife in *Born Yesterday*, Laurence Olivier's production, and he was knighted while we were playing at the Garrick after touring. There'd been such rubbish in the theatre throughout the war – people on leave would put up with anything in order to forget the world for a few hours. This production was easy to look at and had laughs every line – a great success. Restrictions were still very hard, though: to conserve light and heat, instead of the regular evening performance shows went on at five o'clock, and although we were sold out there were no matinées. People still came bundled up in rugs and sat with their coats on. After the play had run for a year we had to get out as the theatre had been booked before we came in by the owner, Jack Buchanan. The week we finished I finally paid off my debts, since I hadn't worked for a year before this engagement.

For a few weeks I taught drama at Brunelleschi's Dance Studio between jobs. I can see how easy it would be to get involved with teaching. I found those weeks totally absorbing. Most of my class were in shows; a couple were models. Mme Brunelleschi wanted them to learn to speak lines and how to walk – just walk. They have to learn to do the lot now, and it's not easy – dancers are afraid to speak.

Our first session, I gave them the paralysing experience of an audition for a straight play – the way it is. Having collected an armful of books, I handed one to each student and asked them to stand in the middle of the

1950: B.L. as the Laughing Woman in Death Of A Salesman, *with Kevin McCarthy and Paul Muni, directed by Elia Kazan at the Phoenix Theatre, London*

Above: *B.L. leaving the Cambridge Theatre, where she played an American tourist in John Osborne's* West Of Suez. *Right: at the Theatre Royal, Drury Lane in* Gone With The Wind, *1972. From left: June Ritchie as Scarlett O'Hara, B.L. as Aunt Pitti-pat, Petra Siniawski as India Wilkes*

room and read a short extract on sight. That way they'd know what to expect if they were asked to do an acting auditon. They would know nothing of the play, the character, its age, type or nationality. And I wanted them to experience, in one week, everything involved in the production of a play as in rep: chalking the layout of the set on the floor, learning to read stage directions, and so on. A rough model made out of match-boxes approximated the designer's conception of the set, which I knew they wouldn't have seen before. Everyone's accent being different, from cockney to Oxford, bothered me not at all – I wanted to shake them up inside, learn to express themselves, open their minds.

More recently, in 1971, I appeared in John Osborne's play *West Of Suez*, first at the Royal Court, and then at the Cambridge Theatre, with Sir Ralph Richardson and Jill Bennett. *Suez* was not an easy play, and many people came twice in order to take it all in. It was my first experience with four-letter words on stage – not that I spoke them. I just played my usual American Tourist Wife. All the other characters were so twisted, tied up and mixed up that when my ordinary 'husband' (played by John Bloomfield) and I made our gauche, home-grown, old-fashioned middle-western appearance near the end of the play the audience very often gave us a round of applause. They were so relieved to be able to identify with the couple of normal, stupid people putting their foot in it no matter what they said or did. This was just the author's trick – to gentle you into a position the more easily to kick you squarely from behind. Once we left what one critic called 'Osborne's Island', came the revolution and guerilla fighters and explosions popped up all over the place. There were more noise and gunshots in that play than I've heard in the West End – except for *Gone With The Wind* at Drury Lane, which I went straight into in March 1972, rehearsing Aunt Pitti-pat.

We had twice as many people in the cast as in *West Of Suez*, and four times as many stage-hands. We had a horse, Charley, and also his understudy, Nelly. (Unfortunately Charley is no more. Nelly became the principal, with an understudy of her own – Johnnie.) A three-year-old tot who looked more like eighteen months old was changed into a five-year-old right before your eyes, which got a round of applause. In keeping with the laws governing children in the theatre we had half a dozen or so of each in a rota so no one was overworked. And even then they were allowed only a certain number of performances before they had to 'retire'.

The minute anyone said a word once the curtain was up, Gloriana, aged four, pressed her finger to her mouth, making the most diminutive rosebud and the loudest 'Shush!' She was a real pro. Sitting on a ground-sheet to protect her taffeta frock on the stairs beside the Green Room, she was describing her Christmas presents to us in whispers when her music cue came. Christmas was left hanging in mid-sentence as she strode downstairs, pushing aside everyone in her way, and stood waiting with her hand upstretched for Max, the A.S.M., to lead her to the wings for her entrance.

Another night, Zoë, also of the age four group, waiting to go on and sitting in the lap of her chaperone, said to me – and to everyone else passing – 'This is my last performance. But I'll be back to play the big Bonnie' (the age group when Bonnie is older). Her chaperone prompted her to say to me, 'I'll miss you, Aunty Bessie,' which she obediently did. Then with large serious eyes she turned back to her chaperone and said, 'And I'll miss you too, Aunty Joyce.' She learned a hard lesson for one so young. Employment in our profession – Zoë's and mine – is one of casual labour. Soon afterwards the show folded – gone with the wind – and we were both out of work. At least, Zoë was. I was able to work on this book.

In films I'm forever doing tourists, mums, aunts, wives – I've no idea how many times. Such work usually takes a couple of days, no more – they pay my salary, it pays the rent . . . Sometimes small beautiful parts turn up, such as Vanessa Redgrave's screen mother in *Isadora* (1967), the story of Isadora Duncan.

When I went to see Karel Reisz, the director, he said that I was so small and Vanessa so tall, he would be obliged to wait until he saw whom he was getting for the brother and sister. Then he said what they *did* need was someone from California to coach Vanessa with her American accent. She herself had suggested me, since I had already coached her when Tony Richardson, then her husband, produced her in Brecht's *St Joan Of The Stockyards* at the Queens Theatre in London.

Karel continued wooing: while the money wouldn't be up to my film salary, I could think of it as a holiday, he said. My companions would be charming (even the tiny parts were to be played by top ranking supporting actors). We would be in Jugoslavia, staying at the best hotels . . .

The hours were pretty horrific – they always have to be on location, where you fight the weather the whole time. But there were rest days: once the whole company was taken in mini-buses over the border to Trieste, another day to Venice! It was like belonging to a club.

A firmly established star, Vanessa Redgrave (V – Nessa – Van – she never minded any of her nicknames) was also an alert, humble student. I hold no degree in speech training – we did it by ear. A few days before shooting started, and practically every waking moment from then on, we read or talked American together. (Throughout my years in London, I have paid trained speech teachers a great deal to *lose* my American accent!) On the way to location at seven a.m., and while she was being made up and her hair dressed, we talked American. After dinner we often read American newspapers and worked on her dialogue for the next day. I was out of camera-shot but not out of earshot for every word she uttered.

I asked Karel if he really did want me to tell him when anything was not right. You get a lot of expensive equipment rolling and the last thing on earth any sensitive artiste wants, whether before or behind the camera, is to hear some monotonous chirp, 'Bath – short A, not bauth. And skedjule, not shedule.' Only once, at the end of a long, long day, high on a crag

140

With Vanessa Redgrave in Isadora

Above: Sunday, Bloody Sunday, *directed by John Schlesinger features B.L. as a busybody telephone operator.* Below: *B.L. and Richard Crenna in* Catlow, *starring Yul Brynner and directed by Sam Wanamaker, on location in Almeria, Spain, 1971*

above the Adriatic, did Karel threaten me between his teeth, 'We can post-sync it in Elstree!' as I opened my mouth at the end of a take.

Recently, in 1976, I played the cashier in *The Ritz*, filmed at Teddington, with most of the New York cast from Broadway. A screwier film I cannot imagine. All I did was count money – no dialogue – just counted money as it slithered down the chute in my cashier's glass cubicle, while all around me the entire cast chased each other, shot each other, pushed each other into the swimming bath and Rita Moreno did her tap-dancing routine on a chair held aloft by her partners and was then tipped into the pool beside the stage. I called rather shrilly to Dick Lester, the director, 'What am I doing in this scene? I don't know what I'm doing.' Over his shoulder he shouted back, 'Why should you be the only one in the picture to know what you're doing? Go on counting money!'

Do you think times have changed since I joined Mr Griffith?

So you want to act? Three portraits, the one below with director John Schlesinger

Finale

━━━━━━━━━━━━━━━━━━━━━━━━

SO YOU WANT TO ACT? ARE YOU sure? Are you willing to get up at five o'clock in order to stand waiting in the snow, wind, rain or sleet – and remember, if it's that kind of weather, it's still dark – for the first bus to take you to the first underground train to take you to the end of the line to stand in a queue for the early Express Bus, then walk on over the slush or spiky frozen ground in order to get your hair dressed at 7.30 and be made up for your most important emotional scene in the film at 8.30?

If you've been a star and are down on your luck you make guest appearances, playing 'cameos'. You ask the studio if they could possibly – and they would, probably – send a car for you. If not, you either hire a car for appearance's sake, or say, 'Nuts!' and wait in the snow for the bus for the underground for the Express and walk on over the frozen ground to . . .

This is not ancient history. Whatever the year, it's always happening, if you want to go into acting, or stay in it. My long journey as a Hollywood climber is typical.

You are invited out by the chief executive from New York who is visiting the West Coast to look things over. A big-name party is being given for him on somebody's private yacht, spending the weekend at Catalina. Your best friends will all be there (it's a very big boat). You pack your bags, kiss your mother goodbye, open the door and the telephone rings. There follows a moment – a long moment – of hesitation: whether to answer, or go before you are told what it is that will stop you? Your mother answers. Yes. The studio. Sadly you pick up the phone.

Hello? This is Miss Glamour-Puss. (Pause.) But the film is finished! (Pause.) But there *are* no re-takes! (Pause.) Mr New York has seen it and says there are? (Pause.) But they're giving a party for him at Catalina and he's expecting me. Can't we do it Monday? (Pause.) He wants to see it – finished – Monday? (Pause.) Okay. See you nine o'clock . . .

145

You shouldn't be depressed. In London the call would be 8.30 – don't ask me why.

Your best friend – a well-known star – is getting married again, and naturally you want to be there. You have never missed one of her weddings; you are always a bridesmaid. You plead with the studio to be let off for the afternoon as they are only doing crowd shots. Impossible! says the studio. They are taking your close-ups. Wait and go to her next wedding, they say. So you do, and do.

One day you are truly initiated. You have been through months of unemployment after such over-employment that you had to go away for a rest, and are accepting the 'one day chicken – next day feathers' philosophy of the business when your agent says he wants you to try for the stage. You learn the words for a starring role in a Broadway success and a couple of songs, and you speak the dramatic lines while doing a soft-shoe dance – which you've never done before, incidentally. The play opens on the Coast and – flops.

And still you cannot get a film job. The market is saturated with your pretty-pretty products from an assembly-line studio, and there are no gutsy starring roles suitable for you. By now your name is too big for small parts – you would detract from the stars and the story. But without knowing it, by soft-shoeing on the boards, you have taken your first step – you are growing up – in a new and bigger career than ever.

Next your agent wants to groom you for musical comedy. He books you to appear live on stage between film showings (which, when silent, the operators ran through at great speed in order to get to the live show). For an enormous salary you are to appear in the enormous cinemas in the West Coast cities.

If you have sense enough to pound sand in a rat-hole, you will remember – and think on it often – that until this engagement you were unable to find a job in your profession. You probably won't remember but you should! You should . . .

So, your party piece that you've been doing for years – clowning around, dancing, singing – has been worked into a small revue with supporting company, by a West Coast touring organization. You do clog, tap, ballroom and eccentric dances; a ventriloquist bit playing the dummy, with a false moustache anchored up your nose; sketches; anything they'll allow you to do to acquire stage experience. Your partner is your playmate from the play which just folded. He works with you as a friend – but as a friend he does everything he can to 'break you up', so that you will learn to take care of yourself when an enemy does the same, trying to ruin your act.

You will not have much time to yourself during this tour of sixteen weeks, because you give four shows a day every day except Saturdays, Sundays and all holidays, when you give five. Saturday night you finish the show; wardrobe and props are packed as each 'spot' is completed; you make a dash for the midnight train; arrive Sunday morning at the new

146

theatre for band call (rehearsal with the resident band); send your dresser out for some sandwiches, and give five shows.

You get married, and one day discover that you are expecting your first baby. Ignorant of this glad news, you have already signed a not-too-bad eight-weeks' contract as a headliner with top billing above star comics, continental acrobats and first-class performers, on a number one vaudeville circuit, with a really stunning act.

In part of your act you are to appear in spangled tights for a stomp-cum-boogie-cum-beat jazz dance of the day, three times a day, seven days a week. And it is July. Your doctor gives you the names of specialists in each of the eight cities where you will appear – just in case.

One week in the Mid-West the theatre air-conditioning gives out. The next week your dresser does not turn up – foolishly you have not travelled with one – and you make a strip change in the middle of the stage, at the footlights, just behind the closed front tabs which open on cue at the end of a mean eight-bar intro to 'St Louis Blues'. And you make it.

In Boston you arrive for band call; instead, as you enter the stage door they yell, 'You're on!' Since the theatre baggage has not yet arrived, you walk on stage in your tailored suit and orchids and tell the Early Bird (eleven a.m.) matinée that you will be with them by the time the film is over. And you are: tights, eyelashes and all.

One night in Chicago you meet an old beau for supper after the show, and, like Cinderella, forget to look at the clock; suddenly you realize you may have to go home in a pumpkin. The station porters assure you there's no need to hurry, because *that* train must have left five minutes ago. You fly down the platform and land in the arms and cheers of the entire company, who are refusing to board the train. The poor guard is throwing the book at them, but they will not budge, knowing that you would never – while alive – let them down.

It's not a boring life. Some people find it a little harrowing . . . You are in a play in Ireland. A dear friend telephones from London to say that your mother has passed on in California. When you finally take it in, you comfort London, cable California, get made-up and go on.

Filmography

The Flying Torpedo (Triangle-Fine Arts 1916): John O'Brien (Director), Wm. Christy Cabanne (Director battle scenes), the McCarthy brothers (Special Effects); George W. Hill (Photographer); with John Emerson, Ralph Lewis, Spottiswoode Aitken, Erich von Stroheim.

The Aryan (Triangle-Ince 1916): William S. Hart, Clifford Smith (co-Directors); Joseph August (Photographer); with William S. Hart, Louise Glaum, Charles K. French, Gertrude Claire, John Gilbert.

Acquitted (Triangle-Fine Arts 1916): Paul Powell (Director); John W. Leezer (Photographer); with Wilfred Lucas, Mary Alden, Elmer Clifton, Carmen De Rue.

The Good Bad Man (Triangle-Fine Arts 1916): Allan Dwan (Director); Victor Fleming (Photographer); with Douglas Fairbanks Senior, Mary Alden, Sam De Grasse, George Beranger, Charles Stevens.

Reggie Mixes In (British title **Facing The Music**) (Triangle-Fine Arts 1916): Wm. Christy Cabanne (Director); William E. Fildew (Photographer); with Douglas Fairbanks Senior, Frank Bennett, Joseph Singleton, Wilbur Higby.

The Mystery Of The Leaping Fish (Triangle-Fine Arts 1916): John Emerson (Director); story by Tod Browning; the McCarthy brothers (Special Effects); John W. Leezer (Photographer); with Douglas Fairbanks Senior, A. D. Sears, Charles Stevens, George Hall.

Stranded (Triangle-Fine Arts 1916): Lloyd Ingraham (Director); Frank Urson (Photographer); with De Wolf Hopper, Carl Stockdale, Frank Bennett, Loyola O'Connor, Tom Wilson.

Hell-To-Pay-Austin (British title **Love In The West**) (Triangle-Fine Arts 1916): Paul Powell (Director); John W. Leezer (Photographer); with Wilfred Lucas, Ralph Lewis, Mary Alden, Eugene Pallette, Monte Blue.

Intolerance (Wark Producing Corporation 1916): David Wark Griffith (Director); George Siegmann, W. S. Van Dyke, Joseph Henabery, Erich von Stroheim, Edward Dillon, Tod Browning (Assistant Directors); G. W. Bitzer (Photographer); Karl Brown (Assistant Photographer); with Mae Marsh, Robert Harron, Miriam Cooper, Margery Wilson, Howard Gaye, Constance Talmadge, Alfred Paget, Seena Owen, Lillian Gish, Elmer Clifton, Walter Long, Tully Marshall, Eugene Pallette, *et al*.

A Sister Of Six (Triangle-Fine Arts 1916): Sidney A. and Chester M. Franklin (co-Directors); David Abel (Photographer); with Frank Bennett, Ralph Lewis, Violet Radcliffe, Carmen De Rue.

The Heiress At Coffee Dan's (Triangle-Fine Arts 1916): Edward Dillon (Director); David Abel (Photographer); with Frank Bennett, Alfred Paget, Max Davidson, Lucille Younge.

Nina The Flower Girl (Triangle-Fine Arts 1917): Lloyd Ingraham (Director); Frank Urson (Photographer); with Elmer Clifton, Alfred Paget, Loyola O'Connor, Jennie Lee, Adele Clifton.

A Daughter Of The Poor (Triangle-Fine Arts 1917): Edward Dillon (Director); Philip du Bois (Photographer); with Roy Stewart, Carmel Myers, Max Davidson, George Beranger, Georgie Stone.

Cheerful Givers (Triangle-Fine Arts 1917): Paul Powell (Director); John W. Leezer (Photographer); with Spottiswoode Aitken, Josephine Crowell, Kenneth Harlan, Pauline Starke.

The Sawdust Ring (Triangle-Ince 1917): Paul Powell, Charles Miller (Directors); Clyde de Vinna, Henry Bredesen (Photographers); with Harold Goodwin, Jack Richardson, Josephine Headley, Daisy Dean.

Wee Lady Betty (Triangle-Ince 1917): Charles Miller (Director); Henry Bredesen (Photographer); with Frank Borzage, Charles K. French, Aggie Herring, Walter Whitman.

Pernickety Polly Ann (Triangle-Ince 1917): Charles Miller (Director); Henry Bredesen (Photographer); with Rowland Lee, Walter Whitman, John Lockney, William Ellingford.

The Great Adventure (Pathé 1918): Alice Guy-Blaché (Director); George K. Hollister, John G. Haas (Photographers); with Flora Finch, Donald Hall, Chester Barnett, Florence Short.

How Could You, Caroline? (Pathé 1918): Frederick Thompson (Director); with James Morrison, Henry Hallam, Edna Earl, Dudley Hawley.

Carolyn Of The Corners (Anderson-Brunton Photoplays 1918): Robert T. Thornby (Director); Frank B. Good (Photographer); with Charles Edler, Charlotte Mineau, Eunice Moore, 'Prince' (a dog).

A Little Sister Of Everybody (Anderson-Brunton Photoplays 1918): Robert T. Thornby (Director); Frank B. Good (Photographer); with George Fisher, Joseph J. Dowling, Hector Sarno.

The Dawn Of Understanding (Vitagraph 1918): David Smith (Director); Charles R. Seeling, Max Dupont (Photographers); with John Gilbert, J. Frank Glendon, George A. Williams, George Kunkel.

The Enchanted Barn (Vitagraph 1919): David Smith (Director); Charles R. Seeling (Photographer); with J. Frank Glendon, Joseph Singleton, Ella Wolbert, William T. Horne.

The Wishing Ring Man (Vitagraph 1919): David Smith (Director); Charles R. Seeling (Photographer); with J. Frank Glendon, Jean Hathaway, Claire Du Brey, Truman Van Dyke.

A Yankee Princess (Vitagraph 1919): David Smith (Director); Clyde de Vinna (Photographer); with Robert Gordon, Aggie Herring, Lydia Yeamans Titus, George Pierce.

The Little Boss (Vitagraph 1919): David Smith (Director); Clyde de Vinna (Photographer); with Wallace McDonald, Otto Lederer, Jay Morley, Harry Russell.

Cupid Forecloses (Vitagraph 1919): David Smith (Director); Clyde de Vinna (Photographer); with Wallace McDonald, Dorothea Wolbert, Frank Hayes, Anne Schaefer, Otto Lederer.

Over The Garden Wall (Vitagraph 1919): David Smith (Director); Clyde de Vinna (Photographer); with Otto Lederer, Anne Schaefer, Allan Forrest, Willis Marks.

A Fighting Colleen (Vitagraph 1919): David Smith (Director); Charles R. Seeling (Photographer); with George Kunkel, Jay Morley, Anne Schaefer, Beulah Clark, Charles Spere.

Pegeen (Vitagraph 1919): David Smith (Director); Charles R. Seeling (Photographer); with Edward Burns, Ruth Fuller Golden, Anne Schaefer, Jay Morley, Charles Spere.

Bonnie May (Andrew J. Callaghan Productions 1920): Ida May Park, Joseph De Grasse (co-Directors); Sam Landers (Photographer); with Charles Gordon, Miss Dupont.

The Midlanders (Andrew J. Callaghan Productions 1920): Ida May Park, Joseph De Grasse (co-Directors); King Gray, (Photographer); Al Rogell (Assistant Photographer); with Truman Van Dyke, C. Norman Hammond, Jack Donovan, Lloyd Bacon.

Penny Of Top Hill Trail (Andrew J. Callaghan Productions 1921): Arthur Berthelet (Director); Sam Landers (Photographer); with Wheeler Oakman, Henry de Vere, Raymond Cannon.

The Honor Of Ramirez (Cyrus J. Williams/Pathé 1921): Robert North Bradbury (Director); with Tom Santschi, Ruth Stonehouse.

The Spirit Of The Lake (Cyrus J. Williams/Pathé 1921): Robert North Bradbury (Director); with Tom Santschi, Ruth Stonehouse.

The Swamp (Hayakawa Feature Play Co. 1921): Colin Campbell (Director); Frank D. Williams (Photographer); with Sessue Hayakawa, Frankie Lee, Lillian Langdon, Janice Wilson.

The Sea Lion (Hobart Bosworth Productions 1921): Rowland V. Lee (Director); J. O. Taylor (Photographer); with Hobart Bosworth, Charles Clary, Emory Johnson, Carol Holloway.

The Vermilion Pencil (Robertson-Cole 1922): Norman Dawn (Director); Joseph Dubray (Photographer); with Sessue Hayakawa, Ann May, Sidney Franklin, Thomas Jefferson.

Forget-Me-Not (Louis Burston Productions 1922): W. S. Van Dyke (Director); Arthur Todd (Photographer); with Gareth Hughes, Otto Lederer, Irene Hunt, William Machin.

Night Life In Hollywood (A. A. Maescher Productions 1922): Fred Caldwell (Director); with J. Frank Glendon, Josephine Hill, Gale Henry.

Bulldog Courage (Clinton Productions 1922): Edward Kull (Director); Harry Neumann (Photographer); with George Larkin, Albert MacQuarrie, Karl Silvera, Frank Whitman.

Deserted At The Altar (Phil Goldstone Productions 1922): William K. Howard, (Director); Glen MacWilliams, John Meigle (Photographers); with William Scott, Tully Marshall, Frankie Lee, Barbara Tennant, Eulalie Jensen.

The Village Blacksmith (Fox 1923): John Ford (Director); George Schneidermann (Photographer); with Virginia Valli, William Walling, Harold Goodwin, George Hackathorne, David Butler, Francis Ford.

The Adventures Of Prince Courageous (series) (Anchor 1923): Frederick G. Becker (Director); Hal Mohr (Photographer); with Arthur Trimble (child).

Three Who Paid (Fox 1923): Colin Campbell (Director), William Wellman (asst. director); John Short (Photographer); with Dustin Farnum, Fred Kohler, Frank Campeau, Robert Agnew.

Ghost Patrol (Universal 1923): Nat Ross (Director); Ben Reynolds (Photographer); with George Nichols, Ralph Graves, Max Davidson.

Souls For Sale (Goldwyn 1923): Rupert Hughes (Director); John Mescall (Photographer); with Eleanor Boardman, Mae Busch, Barbara La Marr, Richard Dix, Lew Cody, Aileen Pringle.

Purple Dawn (Charles R. Seeling Production 1923): Charles R. Seeling (Director); Raymond Walker, Vernon Walker (Photographers); with William E. Aldrich, Edward Piel, Bert Sprotte, Priscilla Bonner.

Mary Of The Movies (Columbia/Robertson-Cole 1923): John McDermott (Director); George Meehan, Vernon Walker (Photographers); with Creighton Hale, Marion Mack, Florence Lee, Jack Perrin.

Human Wreckage (T. H. Ince 1923): John Griffith Wray (Director); Henry Sharp (Photographer); with George Hackathorne, Dorothy Davenport, Claire McDowell, Robert McKim, Lucille Ricksen, James Kirkwood.

St Elmo (Fox 1923): Jerome Storm (Director); Joseph August (Photographer); with Barbara La Marr, John Gilbert, Warner Baxter, Nigel de Brulier.

The Eternal Three (Goldwyn Pictures 1923): Marshall Neilan, Frank Urson (Directors); David Kesson (Photographer); with Raymond Griffith, Claire Windsor, Hobart Bosworth, Alec Francis.

Slave Of Desire (Goldwyn Pictures 1923): George D. Baker (Director); John Boyle (Photographer); with Carmel Myers, George Walsh, Wally Van, Edward Connelly.

Gentle Julia (Fox 1923): Rowland V. Lee (Director); G. O. Post (Photographer); with Harold Goodwin, Mary Arthur, Charles K. French, Frank Elliott.

Torment (Maurice Tourneur Productions 1924): Maurice Tourneur (Director); Arthur Todd (Photographer); with Owen Moore, Maud George, Jean Hersholt, Joseph Kilgour.

A Woman On The Jury (Associated First National 1924): Harry O. Hoyt (Director); James C. Van Trees (Photographer); with Sylvia Breamer, Lew Cody, Mary Carr, H. B. Walthall.

Those Who Dance (T. H. Ince Productions 1924): Lambert Hillyer (Director); Sid Hickox (Photographer); with Blanche Sweet, Warner Baxter, Matthew Betz, Robert Agnew.

Dynamite Smith (T. H. Ince Corporation 1924): Ralph Ince (Director); Henry Sharp (Photographer); with Charles Ray, Jacqueline Logan, Wallace Beery, Lydia Knott.

The Silent Watcher (Frank Lloyd Productions 1924): Frank Lloyd (Director); Norbert F. Brodin (Photographer); with Glenn Hunter, Gertrude Astor, Hobart Bosworth, Lionel Belmore.

Sundown (First National 1924): Lawrence Trimble, Harry O. Hoyt (Directors); David Thompson, L. William O'Connell (Photographers); with Roy Stewart, Hobart Bosworth, Charlie Murray, Arthur Hoyt.

Tongues Of Flame (Famous Players-Lasky 1924): Joseph Henabery (Director); Faxon M. Dean (Photographer); with Thomas Meighan, Eileen Percy, Berton Churchill.

The Lost World (First National 1925): Harry O. Hoyt (Director); Willis H. O'Brien (Technical Director); Arthur Edeson (Photographer); with Wallace Beery, Lloyd Hughes, Lewis Stone, Bull Montana, Arthur Hoyt.

Soul-Fire (Inspiration Films 1925): John Robertson (Director); Roy Overbaugh (Photographer); with Richard Barthelmess, Helen Ware, Walter Long, Carlotta Monterey, Harriet Sterling.

New Brooms (Famous Players-Lasky 1925): William de Mille (Director); L. Guy Wilky (Photographer); with Neil Hamilton, Phyllis Haver, Robert McWade, Josephine Crowell.

A Son Of His Father (Famous Players-Lasky 1925): Victor Fleming (Director); Edgar Schoenbaum (Photographer); with Warner Baxter, Raymond Hatton, Walter McGrail, Carl Stockdale.

The King On Main Street (Famous Players-Lasky 1925): Monta Bell (Director); James Wong Howe (Photographer); with Adolphe Menjou, Greta Nissen, Joseph Kilgour, Oscar Shaw, Carlotta Monterey.

The Song And Dance Man (Famous Players-Lasky 1926): Herbert Brenon (Director); James Wong Howe (Photographer); with Tom Moore, Harrison Ford, Norman Trevor.

Lovey Mary (Metro-Goldwyn-Mayer 1926): King Baggot (Director); Ira H. Morgan (Photographer); with William Haines, Mary Alden, Russell Simpson, Eileen Percy, Vivia Ogden.

Young April (De Mille Pictures 1926): Donald Crisp (Director); Peverell Marley, Arthur Miller (Photographers); with Joseph Schildkraut, Rudolph Schildkraut, Bryant Washburn, Dot Farley.

Going Crooked (Fox 1926): George Melford (Director); Charles Clarke (Photographer); with Oscar Shaw, Gustav von Seyffertitz, Edgar Kennedy, Leslie Fenton.

Rubber Tires (British title **Ten Thousand Reward**) (De Mille Pictures 1927): Alan Hale (Director); Robert Newhard (Photographer); with Harrison Ford, May Robson, Junior Coghlan, Erwin Connelly.

A Harp In Hock (British title **The Samaritan**) (De Mille Pictures 1927): Renaud Hoffman (Director); Dewey Wrigley (Photographer); with Rudolph Schildkraut, May Robson, Junior Coghlan, Joseph Striker.

Dress Parade (De Mille Pictures 1927): Donald Crisp (Director); Peverell Marley (Photographer); with William Boyd, Walter Tennyson, Hugh Allan, Maurice Ryan.

The American (or **The Flag Maker**) (Spoor-Blackton 1927): J. Stuart Blackton (Director); J. Marvin Spoor, William S. Adams, Conrad Luperti (Photographers); with Ward Crane, Charles Ray, Evelyn Selbie, J. P. Lockney.

The Matinée Idol (Columbia 1928): Frank Capra (Director); Philip Tannura (Photographer); with Johnny Walker, Lionel Belmore, Ernest Hilliard.

Anybody Here Seen Kelly? (Universal-Jewel 1928): William Wyler (Director); Charles Stumar (Photographer); with Tom Moore, Kate Price, Tom O'Brien, Alfred Allen.

Sally Of The Scandals (FBO 1928): Lynn Shores (Director); Philip Tannura (Photographer); with Allan Forrest, Margaret Quimby, Jerry Miley, Irene Lambert.

The Swell Head (Warner Vitaphone 1928): Bryan Foy (Director); with Eddie Foy Junior, Eugene Pallette, Claude Saunders.

The Broadway Melody (Metro-Goldwyn-Mayer 1929): Harry Beaumont (Director); John Arnold (Photographer); with Charles King, Anita Page, Eddie Dillon, Jed Prouty, Eddie Kane.

The Idle Rich (Metro-Goldwyn-Mayer 1929): William de Mille (Director); Leonard Smith (Photographer); with Conrad Nagel, Leila Hyams, Edythe Chapman, James Neill.

The Hollywood Revue Of 1929 (Metro-Goldwyn-Mayer 1929): Charles Reisner (Director); John Arnold, Irving Ries, Maximilian Fabian, John M. Nickolaus (Photographers); with Marie Dressler, Polly Moran, Buster Keaton, Joan Crawford, Marion Davies, *et al.*

The Girl In The Show (Metro-Goldwyn-Mayer 1929): Edgar Selwyn (Director); Arthur Reed (Photographer); with Raymond Hackett, Edward Nugent, Ford Sterling, Jed Prouty, Nanci Price.

Chasing Rainbows (Metro-Goldwyn-Mayer 1930): Charles Reisner (Director); Ira H. Morgan (Photographer); with Charles King, Jack Benny, George K. Arthur, Marie Dressler, Polly Moran.

They Learned About Women (Metro-Goldwyn-Mayer 1930): Jack Conway, Sam Wood (Directors); Leonard Smith (Photographer); with Mary Doran, Gus Van, Eddie Gribbon, Joseph T. Schenck.

Conspiracy (RKO 1930): Wm. Christy Cabanne (Director); Nick Musuraca (Photographer); with Ned Sparks, Hugh Trevor, Rita La Roy, Bert Moorehouse, Otto Matieson.

Good News (Metro-Goldwyn-Mayer 1930): Nick Grinde (Director); Percy Hilburn (Photographer); with Mary Lawlor, Lola Lane, Gus Shy, Cliff Edwards, Stanley Smith.

See America Thirst (Universal 1930): William James Craft (Director); Arthur Miller, C. Allen Jones (Photographers); with Harry Langdon, George ('Slim') Summerville, Matthew Betz, Mitchell Lewis, Stanley Fields.

Morals For Women (British title **Farewell Party**) (Tiffany 1931): Mort Blumenstock, Wm. Christy Cabanne (Directors); Max Dupont (Photographer); with Virginia Lee Corbin, June Clyde, Conway Tearle, Natalie Moorehead.

I Live Again (Morgan Films 1936): Arthur Maude (Director); Horace Weddon (Photographer); with Noah Beery, John Garrick, Percy Bush.

Atlantic Ferry (American title **Sons Of The Sea**) (Warner 1941): Walter Forde (Director); Basil Emmott (Photographer); with Michael Redgrave, Valerie Hobson, Griffith Jones, Margaretta Scott.

London Scrapbook (Spectator Short Films 1942): Eugene Cekalski, Derrick De Marney (Directors); A. H. Luff (Photographer); with Basil Radford, Leslie Mitchell.

Journey Together (RAF Film Production Unit 1945): John Boulting (Director); Sgt. Harry Waxman (Photographer); with Richard Attenborough, Edward G. Robinson, Jack Watling, Ronald Squire.

The Magic Box (Festival Film Productions 1950): John Boulting (Director); Jack Cardiff (Photographer); with Robert Donat, Maria Schell, Renée Asherson, Laurence Olivier, *et al.*

No Highway (American title **No Highway In The Sky**) (Twentieth Century-Fox 1951): Henry Koster (Director); Georges Périnal (Photographer); with James Stewart, Marlene Dietrich, Glynis Johns, Jack Hawkins, Janette Scott.

The Weak And The Wicked (American title **Young And Willing**) (Marble Arch 1953): J. Lee-Thompson (Director); Gilbert Taylor (Photographer); with Glynis Johns, John Gregson, Diana Dors, Athene Seyler, Sybil Thorndike, Sidney James.

The Barefoot Contessa (Figaro 1954): Joseph Mankiewicz (Director); Jack Cardiff (Photographer); with Ava Gardner, Humphrey Bogart, Edmund O'Brien, Rossano Brazzi, Marius Goring.

Beau Brummel (Metro-Goldwyn-Mayer 1954): Curtis Bernhardt (Director); Oswald Morris (Photographer); with Stewart Granger, Elizabeth Taylor, Peter Ustinov, Robert Morley.

Touch And Go (American title **The Light Touch**) (Michael Balcon Production 1955): Michael Truman (Director); Douglas Slocombe (Photographer); with Jack Hawkins, Margaret Johnston, June Thorburn, Roland Culver.

The Story Of Esther Costello (American title **Golden Virgin**) (Romulus Films 1957): David Miller (Director); Robert Krasker (Photographer); with Joan Crawford, Rossano Brazzi, Heather Sears, Fay Compton, John Loder.

Next To No Time (Montpelier Films 1958): Henry Cornelius (Director); Freddie Francis (Photographer); with Kenneth More, Betsy Drake, Patrick Barr, Roland Culver.

Nowhere To Go (Michael Balcon Production 1958): Seth Holt (Director); Paul Besson (Photographer); with George Nader, Maggie Smith, Bernard Lee, Geoffrey Keen, Andrée Melly.

Too Young To Love (Beaconsfield 1959): Muriel Box (Director); Gerald Gibbs (Photographer); with Thomas Mitchell, Joan Miller, Pauline Hahn.

The Greengage Summer (American title **Loss Of Innocence**) (PKL Pics 1961): Lewis Gilbert (Director); Frederick A. Young (Photographer); with Kenneth More, Danielle Darrieux, Susannah York.

The Roman Spring Of Mrs Stone (Seven Arts 1961): José Quintero (Director); Harry Waxman (Photographer); with Vivien Leigh, Warren Beatty, Jill St John, Lotte Lenya.

The Wild Affair (Seven Arts 1963): John Krish (Director); Arthur Ibbetson (Photographer); with Nancy Kwan, Terry Thomas, Bud Flanagan, Jimmy Logan.

Children Of The Damned (Metro-Goldwyn-Mayer 1963): Anton W. Leader (Director); David Boulton (Photographer); with Ian Hendry, Alan Badel, Barbara Ferris, Alfred Burke.

I Think They Call Him John (Samaritan Films 1964): John Krish (Director); David Muir (Photographer); with Victor Spinetti (as co-narrator).

Promise Her Anything (Seven Arts 1965): Arthur Hiller (Director); Douglas Slocombe (Photographer); with Leslie Caron, Warren Beatty, Hermione Gingold, Keenan Wynn.

Battle Beneath The Earth (Reynolds/Vetter 1967): Montgomery Tully (Director); Ken Talbot (Photographer); with Kerwin Matthews, Viviane Ventura, Robert Ayres.

I'll Never Forget What's 'Is Name (Scimitar/Universal 1965): Michael Winner (Director); Otto Heller (Photographer); with Orson Welles, Oliver Reed, Harry Andrews, Carol White, Wendy Craig, Marianne Faithfull.

Isadora (Universal 1968): Karel Reisz (Director); Larry Pizer (Photographer); with Vanessa Redgrave, Jason Robards Junior, James Fox, Ivan Tchenko, John Fraser.

On Her Majesty's Secret Service (Eon-Danilag Productions 1969): Peter Hunt (Director); Michael Reed (Photographer); with George Lazenby, Diana Rigg, Telly Savalas.

Sunday, Bloody Sunday (Vectia Films 1971): John Schlesinger (Director); Billy Williams (Photographer); with Glenda Jackson, Peter Finch, Peggy Ashcroft, Tony Britton, Maurice Denham.

Catlow (Metro-Goldwyn-Mayer 1971): Sam Wanamaker (Director); Ted Scaife (Photographer); with Yul Brynner, Richard Crenna, Jo Ann Pflug, Leonard Nimoy, Daliah Lavi.

Gulliver's Travels (Valeness/Belvision 1973): Peter Hunt (Director); Alan Hume (Photographer); with Richard Harris.

Cat And Mouse (Associated London Films 1974): Daniel Petrie (Director); Jack Hildyard (Photographer); with Kirk Douglas, Jean Seberg, Sam Wanamaker.

The Ritz (Courtyard Films/Warner 1976): Richard Lester (Director); Paul Wilson (Photographer); with Jack Weston, Jerry Stiller, Kaye Ballard.

Index